More
Crochet
by
Iris Rathbone

Dedicated to Gilbert
and
His Philosophy of Life

Photo left:
Blouse with gilt edging
see page 38

More
Crochet
by
Iris Rathbone

"Solomon's Knot a tie of three
Secure as the Blessed Trinity"

John Bartholomew & Son Ltd. Edinburgh

Published in Great Britain 1972
by John Bartholomew & Son Ltd
Duncan Street, Edinburgh EH9 ITA

London Office
216 High Street
Bromley, Kent BR1 1PW

ISBN 0 85152 907 0

Printed in Great Britain.

Contents

Facts and Information from

The British Museum	London
Victoria and Albert Museum	London
Ashmolean Museum	Oxford
Pitts Rivers Museum	Oxford
National Museum	Copenhagen
National Museum of Ireland	Dublin
The Book of Knowledge Vol I to VIII	Waverly
Oxford Junior Encyclopaedia Vol XI	
Chamber's Encyclopaedia Vol XI	
Memoirs of a Highland Lady	Elizabeth Grant
Knitting	Mary Thomas
The Sacred History Of Knitting (1st & 2nd Editions)	Heinz E Kiewe
The Ashley Book of Knots	Ashley
The Holy Bible	English
The Concise Oxford Dictionary	

Acknowledgments

I wish to thank all Museums for the help they have given me, especially Miss Blackwood and the staff of Pitts Rivers, Oxford; and Messrs Patons for allowing use of their patterns; Mrs Rosemary Pearce for help with the technicalities; Miss June Shand for her patient modelling; my Family and Husband for their help in small ways; and Miss Wendy Parker for typing my manuscript. Photography Suzanne van de Gohm.

Preface

There is so much to be learnt about this very old craft and what can be done with it.

Once again, on purpose, I have avoided Lace work, as being fine, it is also slow: the women of today need a hobby which brings quicker results, and is also more practical.

Many knitters are dropping their needles and taking to the hook, and adapting the same rules to each craft.

I have shown in this book where these rules are the same and where they differ, and also how these two crafts evolved one from the other.

Introduction

Somewhere, somehow, if you search long enough, you will track down the evidence which reveals how something began. The search may take you down many a blind alley, but it all adds to the spice of life.

In the search for the origins of Crochet, so closely connected with its sister craft of Knitting, I found that much had been lost throughout the ages, and one craft had become muddled together with the other. But at last I believe I have proved how the two crafts developed, one from the other.

First, to find the definitions, as laid down in the Concise Oxford Dictionary. KNIT: form (close texture, garments, etc.) of interlooping yarn or thread . . . using two or more slender rods or needles. CROCHET: a form of knitting using only one needle or slender rod, with a hooked end.

With each of these crafts yarn of any combination is used, whether wool, cotton, string or any man-made fibre in use today.

To discover how Ancient Man made his first yarns I went to the Pitts River Museum (Anthropology) Oxford, very near my home, where I spent many hours studying the exhibits and all they could teach me. The way of life nearest to that of the Stone Age man is to be seen among the tribes of New Guinea. Although their clothing is scanty, these very fierce once-cannibalistic people needed pouches and bags in which to carry their arrows and spoils of the hunt. Many samples of these are on exhibition, fashioned from a yarn of bark fibres. Some are made with the fingers.

Others are made with the aid of a needle, very much like our fisherman's needle, and at first glance many of them look like a crochet fabric.

Pictures from Denmark of the hairnet made about 2200 BC, mentioned in my first book reveal that the craft used was 'Sprang', exactly the same as that used to make the bags from New Guinea, the ones made with the aid of a needle.

Miss Blackwood, Assistant Curator of Pitts River Museum, told me how the primitive natives spun their yarn. The bark fibres were rolled under the fingers against the thigh. What a long tedious task that must have been!

Miss Blackwood was the first white person to live with the most violent tribe in all New Guinea, in the thirties, and she often watched the women at their thigh spinning. Before the days of spindles and spinning wheels this must have been the way the first yarns were spun, whether wool, cotton or hair, etc.

Then I thought of the oldest of all crochet combinations, King Solomon's knot and that led me to the Bible. Both in the Old and New Testaments you can find the word 'Knit'; even Eve was supposed to have 'knit' a coat for the serpent.

Other passages in the Bible refer many times to the 'Sack or Sackcloth', knit or woven. Once again the Concise Oxford Dictionary was consulted for its definition—SACK: a name given to a loose type garment of both sexes.

The seamless Robe of Jesus is described as both knit and woven in different chapters, but they all tell of it being made in one piece from the neck down, without a seam.

Then I read the Sacred History of Knitting by Heinz Edgar Kiewe, which confirmed ideas of my own about the beginnings of the two crafts. Later, in the last chapter of this book, I will show you how crochet came first and knitting developed from it. So they are sister crafts of each other.

Legend has it that the Merry Wives of Windsor wore snoods and headdresses made from crocheted lace.

At the Ashmolean Museum, Oxford, I saw a small Dorothy bag in the Tudor collection, worked in double crochet. Made in very fine red and white gilt thread, the two colours form a pattern of fleur-de-lys, worked in a continuous round, without the slip stitch to join the rounds, as we would use it today. When completed it was stitched to a lining and is reputed to have belonged to Queen Anne (1702–1714).

With the permission of the historian in charge, I examined this bag under a magnifying glass, which showed the change in tension, where the bag was worked on at least three times, not easy to detect with the naked eye.

Following the Queen Anne bag, there is a mention of what must have been crochet in the book 'Memoirs of a Highland Lady' published in 1812, the craft used being called Shepherd's knitting, the yarn used being wool.

Mlle. Eleanore Riego, fleeing from the French Revolution in the year 1820, brought her craft to England, together with the name by which we know it today. At this time we also learn of the stitch Treble, not heard of before.

Starvation in Ireland promoted the craft, as a form of famine relief, in both the north and south. One of the first centres from which it spread all over the south was Ursuline Convent, Blackrock, Cork, in the year 1845.

Already a form of famine relief had been established in Northern Ireland, by the wife of the rector of the parish of Carrickmacross, in the year 1820. Lace brought over from Italy had been copied and developed, and with the advent of crochet this was added to the crafts of the home industries, making mostly decorative items, to help the starving women and children in Ireland. Even today the crafts of Carrickmacross lace and Irish Rose Crochet are a big part of the home industries.

Thus the art of crocheting, lost through the ages, was found again, and interest in it grew year by year, not only in the decorative form, but much more for practical use, for which it was first intended.

Useful facts and figures

Imperial Standard measurements are used throughout this book. To convert these into the appropriate metric equivalents, follow the conversion table below.

Weights
1 oz. = 28.35 grammes
4 oz. = 113.4 grammes
8 oz. = 226.8 grammes
1 lb. = 454 grammes
2 lb. 3 oz. (approx.) = 1 kilogramme
N.B. When buying knitting or crochet yarn, a 25-gramme ball of yarn will approximately equal a 1-oz. ball. But as 1 oz. equals slightly over 25 grammes for larger quantities increase the number of gramme balls, e.g. if 12 oz. yarn is required, buy fourteen 25-gramme balls, and if 20 oz. is required, buy 23 25-gramme balls.

Linear measures
1 inch = 2.54 centimetres
6 inches = 15.2 centimetres
1 foot (12 inches) = 30.48 centimetres
1 yard = 0.914 metre (just over 91 centimetres)
1 yard 4 in. (approximately) = 1 metre

Materials

Hooks. Always use the size as instructed, unless you find your own personal tension too tight, then use a size larger. If your tension is looser, use a size smaller.

We now have a standard international size, which will help us all.

INTERNATIONAL STANDARD SIZES	OLD U.K. SIZES		AMERICAN SIZES	
	Wool	Cotton	Wool	Cotton
7·00	2	—	K	—
—	3	—	—	—
6·00	4	—	—	—
5·50	5	—	—	—
5·00	6	—	J	—
4·50	7	—	I	—
4·00	8	—	H	—
3·50	9	—	G	—
3·00	10	3/0	F	2/0
—	11	2/0	E	0
2·50	12	0	D	1
—	13	1	C	2
—	—	—	—	3
2·00	14	1½	B	4
—	—	2	A	5
1·75	15	2½	—	6
—	—	3	—	—
1·50	16	3½	—	7
—	—	4	—	8
1·25	—	4½	—	9
—	—	5	—	10
1·00	—	5½	—	11
—	—	6	—	12
0·75	—	6½	—	13
0·60	—	7	—	14
—	—	7½	—	—

N.B. Australian, Canadian and South African sizes are the same as old U.K. sizes.

Many people don't realize that the rules of knitting and crochet are different, except in a few instances.

In crocheting, as in knitting, you must pay attention to the instructions about yarns and hooks. If you disregard them, and the article you are making is not perfect, it is your own fault. Remember the many ways in which yarns are spun and dyed—that is the reason for the instructions.

Most written instructions explain the make-up of a garment, using the same method as knitting. Oversewing seams are only adaptable where the sides are completely straight. With the scallops as stepping stones, use back stitch through these, which will give straight seams on the right side.

In motif work, you can either crochet together, or sew together, whichever way you prefer.

Never work any alternative pattern, unless you see a picture of the finished garment; every pattern needs its own design, each combination its measurements.

Don't assume that every pattern is tried and tested before publication. In many cases, where you least expect it, this is not so. Also, patterns are designed by humans, not computers. And humans can make mistakes!

The method of working varies with each garment designed. To and fro, up and down, round and round. If the round method is being used to form a square always turn work after each round.

Tensions—the number of stitches measured to make an inch—are very similar in both crafts, but are more awkward in crochet with its many combinations. With the length and width of the individual stitch, the two inch scale as laid down for knitting is not always adequate for crochet. In many cases a three inch scale is needed.

As crochet does not settle down till after at least four inches, make your sample ten inches, to test a piece for your own tension and overall measurements.

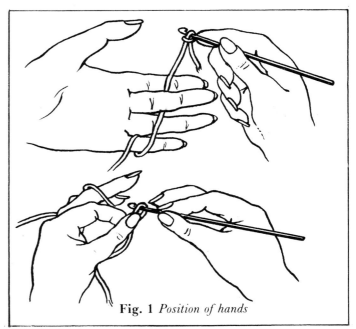

Fig. 1 *Position of hands*

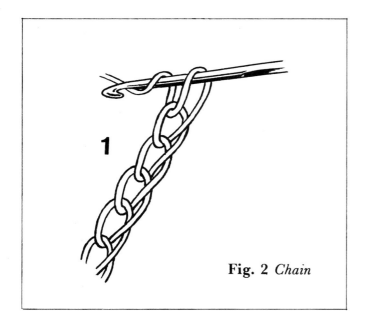

Fig. 2 *Chain*

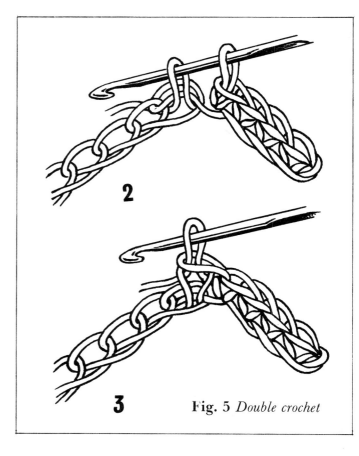

Fig. 5 *Double crochet*

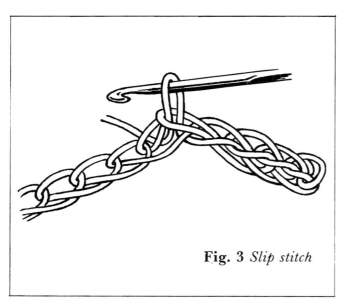

Fig. 3 *Slip stitch*

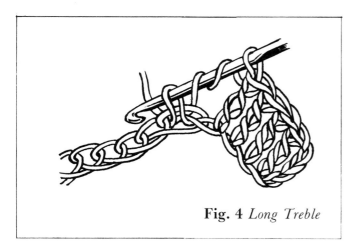

Fig. 4 *Long Treble*

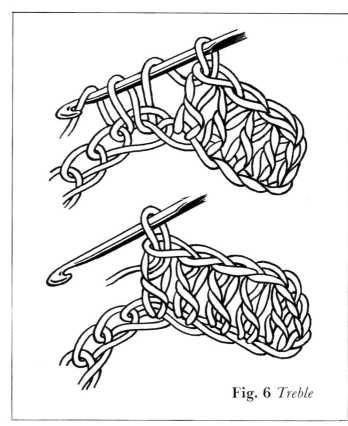

Fig. 6 *Treble*

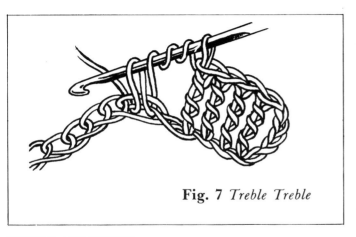

Fig. 7 *Treble Treble*

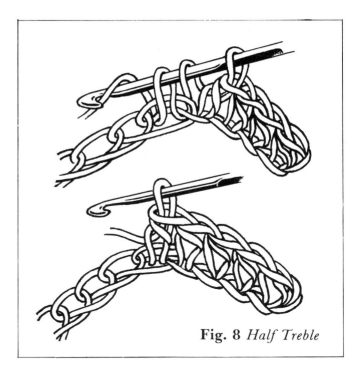

Fig. 8 *Half Treble*

WOOLS AND YARNS

The crochet patterns in this book quote specific brand names and weights of wools and yarns, and for the best results it is recommended that these are used. In some countries the named yarn may not be readily available, but a direct equivalent known by a different brand name is. Where no direct equivalent exists then a standard alternative can often be used. The following chart lists the direct and standard equivalents for yarns quoted in this book. If a yarn does not appear on the chart it can be assumed it is generally available in South Africa, Australia, Canada and USA as well as in the United Kingdom.

U.K.	U.S.A.	S. AFRICA	AUSTRALIA	CANADA
PATONS				
Brilliante Double Knitting	standard d.k.	same	Baroners Double Crêpe	Beehive Astra, pr Sparkella
Double Knitting	standard d.k.	same	Katie Crochet and Totem	Canadiana Knitting Worsted or Beehive Astra
Limelight Quickernit	standard 4-ply	101 Courtelle Quickernit		Carefree Baley Sayelle
Limelight Double Crêpe	standard d.k.	101 Courtelle Double Crêpe	Bonny Courtelle	Limelight Double Crêpe
Fiona	standard 4-ply	Fiona	Totem or Swifta-Knit Bri-Nylon	Beehive Astra
Promise	—	Promise		
Trident	standard d.k.	Patons Double Knit	Katie Crochet	Canadiana Knitting Worsted
Doublet	standard d.d.k.	Doublet	Skoll	Beehive Craft yarns or Carefree Canadiana Double, Double Knitting
Totem Double Crêpe	standard d.k.	Totem	Totem	Canadiana Knitting Worsted or Beehive Astra
HAYFIELDS				
Nylon	—	same		
Croft Double Knitting	standard d.k.			
Brig Aran Type Yarn	standard d.k.			
Beaulon 4-ply Fingering	standard 4-ply	High Crimp Bri-Nylon 4-ply	Standard 4-ply	Courtier 4-ply
Gaylon Double Knitting	standard d.k.			
SIRDAR				
Double Crêpe	standard d.k.	Double Crêpe or Gold Seal Courtelle	Double Crêpe or Gold Seal Courtelle	standard d.k.
Courtelle Crêpe	standard d.k.	Double Knitting or Double Crêpe	Rapsody or Double Crêpe	standard d.k.
LISTERS				
Lavenda Double Knitting	as for U.K.	as for U.K.	standard d.k.	standard d.k.
ROBIN				
Tricel-Nylon Perle	standard 4-ply	standard 4-ply	standard 4-ply	standard 4-ply
Bri-Nylon Super Crimp Double Knitting	standard d.k.	standard d.k.	standard d.k.	standard d.k.

Important Note. Where an exact equivalent yarn given in a pattern is not available the substitute may not give precisely the same measurements, it is therefore important to make a tension check before beginning. Yardage also varies with different yarns and you may find you need either more or less than the quantity specified in the pattern.

Basics

The intricacy of crochet is so very fascinating that the more you know the more you want to know —to improve your craft, and get away from that primitive look seen so much in the work of today.

Chain is the foundation of all work. So what should you learn about it? In some of the fine lace work a double chain was used. It is rather tedious to form and is not needed in modern fashion, so we will ignore it.

That first chain will have its tendency to tightness, and how aggravating that can be. To overcome this, make that first chain loose. If, when the garment is completed, you are not satisfied with the edge, work a round of double crochet, which will form a binding.

With no pin to hold the number of stitches, the counting can be irritating. Remembering that the loop on the hook is not counted, have a few small safety pins handy. After each twenty chain place a pin, so that if you lose count you have only to go back to a pin. The number of basic chain given are not your working stitches, as the last few are needed to draw your work to the level of the next row.

Confusion has arisen in many quarters about the chain turn, and how to keep your sides straight. When working in the round, the chain turn always replaces the first stitch. This is not so when working to and fro; the chain turn can replace the first stitch, and in other cases is only the means of drawing your starting loop to the height of the next row. It depends on what combination of stitches is being used for the individual design.

If making a square, try to start each round in the corner if possible; your chain then blends in and no join shows.

There is no simple rule for keeping your sides straight, and you can only get this right by watching very carefully what you are doing. In knitting, having a guide with the two needles taking one stitch from the left to the right enables the worker to read at the same time. With crochet your eyes need to be kept on your work, as you have no guide to help the entry.

Slip stitch or single crochet, is a very tight stitch not generally used as a progressive working stitch, but very useful in all shapings. When using it for these, work it loosely.

Enter work, draw yarn through, both work and loop on hook leaving one loop.

Double Crochet, enter work, draw yarn through, making 2 loops on the hook, yarn round hook, draw through these two loops.

Treble, always place yarn round hook before entry into work, draw yarn through making three loops on the hook, to be worked off in 2's in the same manner as double crochet.

Four basic stitches, from which everything in crochet evolves, lengthened, shortened, combined, which make further stitches and beautiful patterns.

Long or Double Treble, is worked in the same manner as treble, only placing the yarn twice round the hook before entry into stitch. This lengthens and makes 4 loops to be worked off in 2's.

Triple or Treble Treble, lengthened even further, making 5 loops on the hook to be worked off in 2's.

To get a stitch in between the height of treble, and double crochet, the basic treble is shortened, giving us short or half treble. Made as treble till 3 loops are on the hook, then yarn round hook, draw through all 3 loops.

Basic Stitches *(see pages 12 and 13)*

A cluster or tuft is two or more trebles worked together, mostly into the same place, and retaining the last loop of each stitch on the hook. When the number is made, the yarn is then placed round the hook and drawn through all loops.

In a similar manner the bobble is formed, working in short treble, retaining all loops on the hook till you have the number required, and then yarn round hook, drawing through all loops.

Once you have learnt all the basic stitches, then you must learn all the entries and what can be done with them.

How many are there? you may well ask. One number quoted is eight plus one—chain space, between stitches, standard, stem, front loop, back loop, forward and back, the plus one being tunisian.

When searching through many patterns and books over the years others have been found, which are used and have been used for a long time, giving many different effects to the finished fabric.

Garments of other entries in this book, have been made up with my designs, to show what can be done, and how much more can be achieved with them.

The quickest two are the chain space entry

and between stitch entry. Using these the work grows rapidly.

Making Grandma's Traditional squares, the best point at which to start crochet, your work will soon be finished and you will feel satisfied you are getting somewhere.

I would point out that this is one of the times when the chain needs to be left out, only used at the corners. A space will be left between each block along the sides for entry on the next round.

After each round of your work, turn it completely if you wish to keep your square, otherwise your square will pull further and further out after every round.

Compare a knitted stitch with your crochet stitch; the knitted stitch has its threads from each side and a loop in the middle.

Fig. 9 *Drawing of a knitted stitch*

A crochet stitch has 2 threads from the right, making the loops and finishing on the left.

Fig. 10 *Drawing of a crochet stitch*

You will always get a pull to the left no matter what stitch you are working. When going to and fro this draws first to one side and then the other, ending even. This is why you need to turn your work where a square is needed, as no amount of pressing will overcome this.

If you are making a round shape there is no need to turn.

The next entry is the standard entry, your finished stitch always falling to the left of the one below; this is used when no other is indicated.

Fig. 11 *Drawing of Standard Entry*

Your stitches can fall directly on each other, if you use the Stem Entry, which will also make a great deal of difference to all shell patterns.

When working in trebles only, using this method of entry, you obtain a neater, flatter, firmer fabric, and you will find it easier to see and keep your side straight.

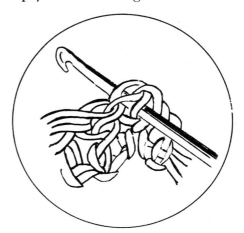

Fig. 12 *Drawing of Stem Entry*

Abbreviations

All garments have to be abbreviated in written instruction, and by now are probably becoming familiar to you; study the list and meanings before going any further.

Chain	ch	Basic Stitch
Double Crochet	dc	Basic Stitch
Slip Stitch Single Crochet	ss	Basic Stitch
Treble	tr	Basic Stitch
Half or Short Treble	s tr h tr	Basic Stitch Shortened
Long Treble Double Treble	l tr d tr	Basic Stitch Lengthened
Triple or Treble Treble	t tr	Basic Stitch Lengthened More
Yarn round hook Yarn on Hook	yrh yoh	Movement
Draw yarn through	dyt	Movement
Loop	lp	Forming
Space	sp	hole or opening
Stem	stm	Upright bar of stitch
Increase	inc	Add
Decrease	dec	Take Away
Stitch/s	st/s	
Together	tog	
Forward	fwd	Entry Front
Back	bk	Entry Back
Block	blk	Combination
Knot	k	Combination
Cluster	cl	Combination
Cross	C	Combination
Long Cross	l c	Combination
Group	gr	Combination
Shell	sh	Combination
Bobble	B	Combination
Picot	P	Combination
Pattern	Patt	Fabric finish
Repeat	rep	
Centimetres	cm	
Approximately	approx	
Main Shade	m.s.	
Contrast	c	

Little boys' jumper, one row under entry.

Little girls' dress, continuation of the feather pattern.

Armbag, a little bit different.

Hooded jacket using treble back

Increase and Decreasings

Shaping is formed by missing stitches or working stitches together, varying with each pattern used. Where you are working in only one basic stitch, it seems simple; when working in combinations, and keeping a continuation of pattern, many problems arise. With so little space available for written instruction, much has to be guesswork.

To increase, you work twice into one stitch, exactly the same as the other craft. In the same manner, the number can be 3 or 4, depending always on the pattern and what is hoped to be achieved with the garment on hand.

Looking very carefully at the drawing of the single stitch, and noting the pull to the left, you must shape either on each row, or on every third row, and not on every alternative, and then the pull will even itself out, first to one side, then to the other.

Increasing each end of the work, if the turn replaces the first stitch, work twice into the second, and twice into the last.

Where a number of stitches are required at the ends of your work, you add chain, allowing extra for the turn. At the same time, work the extra stitches on an odd piece of yarn, to be added on after the row, giving an increase at the same level each side.

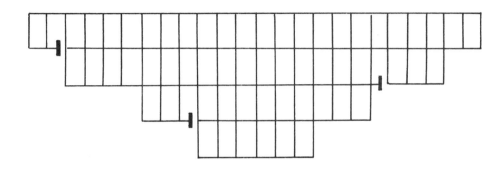

Fig. 13 *Diagram of Increase*

Each square represents 1 stitch, the broken square at the end showing where the extra stitches are added at the ends of the row.

In the same way as in knitting, where a tailored sleeve is required, the extra stitches are best increased in ones each side of the rows, worked in the main stitch till enough have been added to form the pattern.

Decrease and its many problems, and ways it can be done. Miss a stitch, something to be avoided at all costs in the sister craft, yet often used in crochet. Not only for decreases, also in the pattern combination.

When using the miss a stitch method at the beginning of a row, make the turn, enter second stitch. If the turn replaces the first stitch, enter third stitch.

At the other end, you can either work to within the last 2 stitches, miss 1 stitch and work the last, or miss the last one altogether.

In producing a garment such as a dress, the best method is to work the decreases as darts, and avoid the miss a stitch at the outside seams, which make stepping stones. So many designs are spoiled because of the clumsy and untidy seams, which could be eliminated if darts were worked.

To increase one stitch, two stitches are worked together. Form the 2 stitches to the last phase, retaining last loops on the hook, yarn round hook, and draw through all loops. This method is worked also over 3 stitches, leaving 1 working stitch, making a decrease of 2.

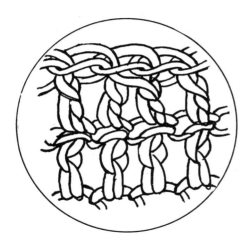

Fig. 14 *Drawing of decrease*

Slip stitch, a term used in both crafts, meaning different things for each one. A number of stitches can be decreased at the beginning of a row by slip stitching along them to the number desired.

To obtain a decrease on the other side on the same level, work to within a given number of stitches, turn work the return row.

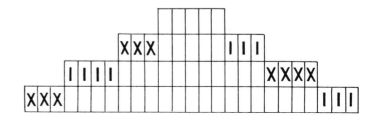

Fig. 15 *Diagram of decrease each end.*
The line down indicating—slip stitch.
The cross "work to within".

Fig. 16 *Dart One*

Dart one, which can be used in many garments uses the missing method; here a block of 2 stitches has been missed on each third row.

Fig. 17 *Dart Two*

Dart two, a combination of worked decreases has been used.

Often the half shell decrease is called for, which confuses many. If the shell is made of 3, 5, 7, 9 stitches, you slip stitch along to the centre which is the 2, 3, 4, 5th stitch and work from there.

An exercise in increasing and decreasing, using the work together method, is the simple tie shown below. It will work out in any double type yarn and an Aero 3.50(9) hook. The one shown is made in Lister Lochinvar double knitting, which gives an interesting effect.

Man's Tie

Ch 3 sts. Work 3 s-tr's into first.
Working in s-trs throughout. Increase into the first and last st, to 9 working sts.

1st row. Increase into first st, decrease over last 2 sts.

2nd row. Decrease over first 2 sts, increase into last st.

Work in this manner for 17 inches, from short point.

For one row only, omit first increase and decrease over 3 sts at the end. Work the pattern 2 rows, for 48 inches when slightly stretched. Over next 4 rows, omit the increase. Cast off and sew in ends.

The man's pullover is made by using decreasings and increasings at the ends of the rows.

see pattern on page 32

Fig. 18 *Picture of Tie*

More entries
and what they can do

In the working of fine cotton, the whole range of entries is not used. Mostly chain space and standard. As the work is very much finer, the stitches appear to fall exactly on each other, and the threads do not show up as clearly as when working in thicker yarn.

By combining all the entries ever used in wool type work many interesting and different fabrics can be achieved.

Instead of entering under the 2 threads at the top of your work enter under the back thread. This will give you a ridged effect, more pronounced if the stitch used is double crochet (see cushion made in small squares of different colours.)

On exhibition at Pitts Rivers Museum is an old Turkish Purse from Cyprus, worked in a continuous round using the back loop entry. It is worked in colour, which forms a pattern of water vessels.

Although the finished fabric is close and unusual it is not suitable for making a garment because it would stretch. It has been used very successfully lengthwise, which needs a binding edge.

Two cushions

(see full colour illustrations facing page 49)

The yarn used when making the cushions and the arm bag, was by Hayfield, a Nylon sold in ounce hanks, very cheaply.

To make the ridge square cushion, 3 ounces of main and 3 ounces of contrast. Number 3.50(9) hook.

Ch 17 sts, ldc into each from 2nd. 1 ch turn.
15 rows more of dc's entering into back 1 p.
9 squares of each colour, sewn together on wrong side, with the line of fabric turned against each other.
The long chain sewn on after.
With the two large squares, finish off by working 3 rows of s-tr, turning after each round, working twice into the corners.
Join the two sides together with a sh, 3 s-tr and 1 dc between sh, 5 s-tr's into corners. Leave an opening one side for the stuffing.

Working into the front loop also forms a ridged finish, not so pronounced.

Alternating the front and back loop entries, with known ones, results in something again different.

Fig. 19 *Use of back loops*

Ch 25 sts.
Foundation. Into 3rd ch from hook, 2 tr.
* miss 1 st, ldc into back 1p, miss 1 st, 3 tr into next * end row with ldc.
Pattern row. 3 ch for the turn and first st. Into dc–2tr.
* ldc into back loop of 2nd Tr of sh, into dc–3tr ending with dc.

Cushion made in two squares, see picture, using the back loop entry. Using 4 ounces of main and 3 ounces of contrast, thick spun double knitting, and a Number 3.50(9) Aero hook. Remember when working in the round the rule applies that the first chain always replaces the first stitch. 4 ch, ss to form the ring.

1st round

3 tr-1ch, 4 times into ring ss to join.
After every round completely turn work.

2nd round

Under 1 ch sp, 3 tr-1ch-3tr (form corner) into 2nd tr of 3-1 dc into back lp. Repeat all round.

3rd round and every round

Into corner ch sp, 3tr-1ch-3tr, * 3 tr into dc, into 2nd tr of 3, 1 dc bk lp *.

After 4 rounds change to 2 contrast, 2 main, 2 contrast, 2 main, 2 contrast, 2 main.

Make 2 sides, and join together by crocheting a shell, 3 tr into dc, 1 dc into middle of 3 and 5 tr's at corner, leave an opening one side for stuffing.

Fig. 21 *Using front and back loop entry*

Ch 29 sts.
Foundation row. Into 3rd st from hook ltr, * ldc-ltr * along row.

1st row. Turn with 3 ch. * 1 tr into previous tr-1 dc into back lp of dc. Ending 1 tr.

2nd row turn. * 1 tr into tr. 1 dc front lp of dc * ending 1 tr.

Scarf

(see full colour illustration facing page 33)

Yarn required will be a little over double for a stole, as the fringe uses up a good deal.
8 balls, each ¾ ounces, of Robin Tricel Nylon Perle. Milwards 3.00(11) hook.

Measurements: Length 60 inches approximately without a fringe width 12 inches approximately.

Tension approximately. 1 row ¾ inch. 1 pattern 1½ inches. Ch 86 sts for the scarf or 166 sts for stole (stole not shown). 1 dc into each st, starting at 2nd from hook.

Foundation row. 1 ch * miss 4 sts, 1 sh into next st (sh, 1 ltr-1ch 1 ltr-1ch-1 ltr-1ch-1 ltr-1ch-1 ltr) miss 4 sts, ldc into bk lp of next * working half a sh into last st.

Pattern row. 1 ch, * into ldc-1sh, into bk lp of 3rd ltr, ldc *. Repeat * * ending with half sh.
Continue straight till work measures 60 inches. Cast off.
The best method of joining yarn is by splicing.
Add fringe to any length desired.

Fig. 20 *A Shell with front and back loop*

Ch 27 sts, and foundation row. Into 4th ch from hook, 5tr, * miss 2 sts, 1 dc into top loop, miss 2 sts, 5 tr * ending row with ldc.

1st row. 1ch turn also represents first st. * into stem of 3rd tr of sh-5 tr, into front lp of dc-ldc *.

2nd row. 3 ch 2 tr into dc. * Into 3rd tr of sh, ldc back lp, into dc 5tr. * Ending row with 3 tr into last dc.

3rd row. 3 ch 2 tr into 1st tr. * ldc into front lp of dc, 5 tr into stem of 3rd tr of sh.

4th row. 1 ch, into dc, 5 tr, into bk lp of 3rd tr ldc.

Little Girl's Tunic

Materials: 3, [3, 4] balls (50 gram) Patons Double Knitting. Crochet Hook No. 7 (4.50mm), No. 8 (4.00mm) and No. 9 (3.50mm). 2 hooks and eyes for Belt.

Measurements: To fit chest 22 [24, 26] in. (56 [61, 66] cm). Length from top of shoulders, 14 [15½, 17] in. (36 [39, 43] cm).

Tension: 2 patts. and 5½ rows to 2 in. (5 cm) With No. 8 hook, make 47 [51, 55] ch.

BACK AND FRONT ALIKE

With No. 8 hook, make 47 [51, 55] ch.

1st row—(Wrong side), 1 d.c. in 2nd ch. from hook, 1 d.c. in each st. to end, turn with 1 ch. (46 [50, 54] sts.).

2nd row—1 d.c. in each st. to end, turn with 1 ch.

3rd row—As 2nd row.

Change to No. 7 hook and work in **patt.** as follows:—

1st row—1 d.c. in each of next 2 sts., * 4 ch., miss 2 d.c., 1 d.c. in each of next 2 sts., rep. from * to end, turn with 5 ch.

2nd row—2 d.c. in first ch. sp., * 4 ch., 2 d.c. in next ch. sp., rep. from *, ending 2 ch. 1 tr. in last st., turn with 1 ch.

3rd row—1 d.c. in first st., 1 d.c. in first ch. sp., * 4 ch., 2 d.c. in next ch. sp., rep. from *, ending last rep., 1 d.c. in last ch. sp., 1 d.c. in 3rd of 5 ch., turn with 5 ch.

2nd and 3rd rows form patt.

Continue in patt. until Back measures 6 [7, 8] in. (15 [18, 20] cm).

Change to No. 8 hook and continue in patt. until Back measures 9 [10, 11] in. (23 [25, 28] cm), ending with a 3rd patt. row, and omitting turning ch. on last row.

Shape armholes as follows:—

1st row—s.s. over 2 d.c., then over 1 ch., 1 ch., 2 d.c. in ch. sp., (4 ch., 2 d.c. in next ch. sp.) 10 [11, 12] times, turn.

2nd row—s.s. over 2 d.c., then over 1 ch., 1 ch., 2 d.c. in ch. sp., (4 ch., 2 d.c. in next ch. sp.) 9 [10, 11] times, turn with 5 ch.

3rd row—s.s. over 2 d.c. then over 1 ch., 1 ch., 2 d.c. in ch. sp., (4 ch., 2 d.c. in next ch. sp.) 8 [9, 10] times, turn with 5 ch.

Shape neck as follows:—

4th row—2 d.c. in first ch. sp., (4 ch., 2 d.c. in next ch. sp.) twice, turn.

5th row—s.s. over 2 d.c., then over 1 ch., 1 ch., 2 d.c. in ch. sp., 4 ch., 2 d.c. in next ch. sp., 4 ch., 1 d.c. in last ch. sp., 1 d.c. in 3rd of 5 ch., turn with 5 ch.

Continue straight in patt. on these sts. for first side until Back measures 14 [15½, 17] in. (36 [39, 43] cm), omitting turning ch. on last row.

Fasten off.

With right side facing, leave centre 2 [3, 4] ch. sp. unworked, rejoin yarn to next ch. sp. and work 2 d.c. in this ch. sp., patt. to end.

Finish to correspond with first side reversing shaping.

(MAIN PIECE)

Belt

With No. 9 hook, make 8 ch.

1st row—1 d.c. in 2nd ch. from hook, 1 d.c. in each ch. to end, turn with 1 ch. (7 sts.).

2nd row—1 d.c. in each st. to end, turn with 1 ch.

Rep. last row until Belt measures 19 [21, 23] in. (48 [53, 58] cm) or required length, omitting turning ch. on last row.

Fasten off.

(CENTRE PIECE)

With No. 9 hook, make 4 ch., join in a ring with s.s. in first ch.

1st round—3 ch., 11 tr. into ring, join with s.s. in top of 3 ch. (12 sts.).

2nd round—3 ch., 1 tr. in base of 3 ch., 2 tr. in each st. to end, join with s.s. in top of 3 ch. (24 sts.).

Fasten off.

TO MAKE UP

With wrong side of work facing, press each piece lightly using a warm iron and damp cloth.

Tunic

Using a flat seam, join shoulder and side seams. With right side facing and No. 9 hook, work 2 rounds d.c. all round neck edge and each armhole. Press seams.

Belt

Sew one end of Belt to centre of Centre Piece. Sew hooks to one end of Belt and eyes to other end.

(Paton's pattern)

Matinee Coat and Bonnet

Materials: Of Patons Limelight Quickerknit 3 balls (25 gram) in Main Shade and 1 ball (25 gram) in Contrast for Coat. 1 ball (25 gram) each in Main Shade and Contrast for Bonnet.
Crochet hook No. 9 (3.50 mm).
Length of ribbon for Coat and Bonnet.
Measurements: To fit 18-19 in. (46-48 cm) chest. Length from top of shoulders, 9 in. (23 cm) excluding picot edging.
Sleeve seam, 5 in. (13 cm) excluding picot edging.
Tension: 12 trs. and 5½ rows to 2 in. (5 cm)
Abbreviations: Cl.=work cluster as follows:— (y.r.h., draw loop through next st.) 4 times all in same st., y.r.h., and draw loop through all 9 loops on hook, 1 ch.
Note: 3 ch. at beg. of tr. rows counts as 1 st. and 1 ch. on d.c. rows does **not** count as a st.

COAT

Starting at neck edge in M.S., make 54 ch.
1st row—1 tr. in 4th ch. from hook, 1 tr. in every following ch. to end, turn.
Break M.S.
2nd row—Join in C., 1 ch., 1 d.c. in each of first 3 sts., * 2 d.c. in next st., 1 d.c. in each of next 2 sts., rep. from * to last 4 sts., 2 d.c. in next st., 1 d.c. in each of last 3 sts. (68 sts.), turn.
Break C.
3rd row—Join in M.S., 3 ch., miss 1st st., * 1 Cl. in next st., 1 ch., miss next st., rep. from * to last st., 1 tr. in last st., turn.
Break M.S.
4th row—Join in C., 1 ch., 1 d.c. in first st., * 1 d.c. in ch. sp., 1 d.c. in top of Cl., rep. from * to last st., 1 d.c. in top of 3 ch., turn.
Break C.
5th row—Join in M.S., 3 ch., miss first st., 1 tr. in each of next 3 sts., * 2 tr. in next st., 1 tr. in each of next 3 sts., rep. from * to end, turn (84 sts.).
6th row—3 ch., miss first st., 1 tr. in each of next 3 sts., * 2 tr. in next st., 1 tr. in each of next 4 sts., rep. from * to end, turn (100 sts.).
7th row—3 ch., miss first st., 1 tr. in each of next 3 sts., * 2 tr. in next st., 1 tr. in each of next 5 sts., rep. from * to end, turn (116 sts.).
Divide for Left Front as follows:—
1st row—(Right side), 3 ch., miss first st., 1 tr. in each of next 14 sts., 3 tr. in next st., 1 tr. in each of next 7 sts., turn.

2nd row—3 ch., miss first st., 1 tr. in each st. to end, but working 3 tr. in centre tr. of 3 tr. group.
Rep. last row 3 times more (33 sts.).
Fasten off.
Continue for **Back** as follows:—
Leaving 13 sts. unworked, with rights ide facing, rejoin M.S. to next st. and make 3 ch., 1 tr. in each of next 6 sts., 3 tr. in next st., 1 tr. in each of next 28 tr., 3 tr. in next st., 1 tr. in each of next 7 sts., turn.
Work 4 rows more in tr., working 3 tr. in centre st. of each 3 tr. group on every row (64 sts.).
Fasten off.
Continue for **Right Front** as follows:—
Leaving 13 sts. unworked, with right side facing, rejoin M.S. to next st. and make 3 ch., 1 tr. in each of next 6 sts., 3 tr. in next st., 1 tr. in each of next 15 sts.
Work 4 rows more as for Left Front.
Fasten off.
Work **Left Sleeve** as follows:—
With right side facing, rejoin M.S. to last row on Left Front and work 3 ch., 9 tr. along armhole edge, work in tr. across 13 sts. of yoke increasing 2 sts. evenly, then 10 tr. down armhole edge of Back (35 sts.).
Work 9 rows in tr. decreasing 1 st. at centre of last row (34 sts.).
Break M.S.
Join in C. and work 1 row in d.c., turn.
Break C.
Next row—Join in M.S., 3 ch., miss 1st st., * 1 Cl. in next st., 1 ch., miss next st., rep. from * to last st., 1 tr. in last st., turn.
Break M.S.
Next row—Join in C., 1 ch., 1 d.c. in first ch. sp., * d.c. in top of Cl., miss 1 ch. sp., rep. from * to last 2 sts., 1 d.c. in next st., turn (17 sts.).
Break C.
Next row—Join in M.S., 3 ch., miss 1st st., 1 tr. in each st. to end.
Fasten off.
With right side facing, join in C. and work **picot edge** as follows:—
Next row—1 d.c. in 1st st., * 1 d.c. in next st., 3 ch. 1 s.s. in same st., 1 d.c. in next st., rep. from * to end.
Fasten off.
Right Sleeve—Work to correspond with Left Sleeve.

Matinee Coat and Bonnet

Continued

Work **Skirt** as follows:—
Rejoin M.S. to right front edge and work 3 ch., 1 tr. in each st. to end, then work in tr. across Back and Left Front (130 sts.), turn.
Work 8 rows more in tr.
Break M.S.
Join in C. and work 1 row of d.c., then breaking off and joining in colours as required, rep. 3rd and 4th rows as at start of Coat then work 1 row in tr.
Fasten off.
With M.S., work 1 row d.c. along each front edge of Coat.

Picot Edge
With right side facing, join in C. to top of Right Front and work as follows:—
* 1 d.c. 3 ch. 1 s.s. all in same st., miss next st., 1 d.c. in next st., rep. from * all round neck, down left front edge, all round lower edge and up right edge.
Fasten off.

TO MAKE UP
With wrong side of work facing, press lightly using a **cool** iron and **dry** cloth.
Join sleeve seams.
Press seams.
Sew ribbon to each front at neck edge.

BONNET
With M.S., make 4 ch., join with s.s. to form a ring.

1st round—3 ch., 9 tr. into ring (10 sts.), join with a s.s. to top of 3 ch. on every round.
2nd round—3 ch., 1 tr. in same st. as s.s., 2 tr. in each st. to end (20 sts.).
3rd round—As 2nd round (40 sts.).
4th round—3 ch., 1 tr. in same st. as s.s., 1 tr. in each of next 4 sts., * 2 tr. in next st., 1 tr. in each of next 4 sts., rep. from * to end (48 sts.).
5th round—3 ch., 1 tr. in same st. as s.s., 1 tr. in each of next 5 sts., * 2 tr. in next st., 1 tr. in each of next 5 sts., rep. from * to end (56 sts.).
6th round—3 ch., 1 tr. in same st. as s.s., 1 tr. in each of next 6 sts., * 2 tr. in next st., 1 tr. in each of next 6 sts., rep. from * to end (64 sts.).
7th round—3 ch., 1 tr. in same st. as s.s., 1 tr. in each of next 7 sts., * 2 tr. in next st., 1 tr. in each of next 7 sts., rep. from * to end (72 sts.).
Work backwards and forwards in rows as follows:-
Next row—3 ch., miss first st., 1 tr. in each of next 2 sts., miss next st., 1 tr. in each of next 4 sts., rep. from * to last 4 sts., miss next st., 1 tr. in each of next 3 sts. (58 sts.).
Work 3 rows in tr.
Break M.S.
Join in C. and work 1 row d.c.
Breaking off and joining in colours as required, rep. 3rd and 4th rows as for Coat.
Next row—In M.S., 3 ch., miss 1st st., 1 tr. in each st. to end.
Fasten off.
With right side facing, join in C. and work picot edge as for Coat round front edge of Bonnet.
With M.S., work 2 rows of d.c. round neck edge.
Cut ribbon in half and sew to each side of Bonnet.

(Paton's pattern)

Child's Dress and Hat

Materials: Dress: 6 [7, 7] balls (1 oz.) Patons Fiona in Dark and 3 [3, 3] balls (1 oz.) in Light. **Hat:** 1 ball (1 oz.) Patons Fiona in Dark and 1 ball (1 oz.) in Light.
No. 8 (4.00mm) and No. 9 (3.50mm) crochet hooks. 3 small buttons for Dress.

Measurements: Dress: To fit 22 [24, 26] in. (56 [61, 66] cm) chest. Length from top of shoulders 16½ [18½, 20½] in. (42 [47, 52] cm). Sleeve seam 1½ [1½, 1½] in. (4 [4, 4] cm).
Hat: To fit Average Head.

Tension: 8 sts. and 4 rows to 2 in. (5 cm) measured over trebles on No. 8 hook.

Note: Turning ch. of previous row counts as 1 stitch, and the first stitch is missed on every row.

DRESS
BACK YOKE

With No. 8 hook and D., make 49 [53 ,57] ch. marking the 23rd [25th, 27th] ch., turn.
** **1st row**—(Right side), 1 tr. in 5th ch. from hook, 1 tr. in each ch. to end, turn with 3 ch. (46 [50, 54[sts.).
2nd row—Miss first st., * 1 tr. in next st., rep. from * ending 1 tr. in top of 3 ch., turn with 3 ch.
Rep. last row once more, omitting turning ch.
Shape armholes as follows:—

Next row—s.s. over 4 sts., 3 ch., patt. to last 4 sts., turn.
Next row—s.s. over 1 st., 3 ch., patt. to last st., turn.
Rep. last row until 32 [36, 40] sts. remain, turn with 3 ch. **
Work straight until Yoke measures 5½ [6, 6½] in. (14 [15, 17] cm), omitting turning ch. on last row, ending with **wrong** side facing.
Shape shoulders as follows:—
Next row—s.s. over 4 [4, 5] sts., 3 ch., patt. to last 4 [4, 5] sts., turn.
Next row—s.s. over 4 [5, 5] sts., 3 ch., patt. to last 4 [5, 5] sts., fasten off.

FRONT YOKE

With No. 8 hook and D., make 49 [53, 57] ch., turn.
Work as for Back Yoke from ** to **.

Work a few rows straight until Yoke measures 4 [4½, 5] in. (10 [11, 13] cm), ending with right side facing.
Divide for neck as follows:—
Next row—Patt. 10 [11, 12], turn.
Next row—s.s. over 2 sts., 3 ch., patt. to end, turn with 3 ch.
Next row—In patt.
Shape shoulder:—
Next row—Patt. 4 [5, 5].
Fasten off.
Leaving centre 12 [14, 16] sts. unworked, rejoin yarn in next st. and finish to correspond with first side, reversing shapings.
Join side seams.

SKIRT
(Worked in one piece)
With right side of Yoke facing, No. 8 hook and D., rejoin yarn in marked st. on Back Yoke.
1st round—3 ch., 2 tr. in st. just worked into, * miss 1 st., 3 tr. in next st., rep. from * all round yoke edge, ending s.s. in top of 3 ch. (46 [50, 54] groups of 3 tr.).
Join in L.
2nd round—In L., 4 ch., 1 tr. in sp. between first and last groups of 3 tr. of previous round, * (1 tr. 1 ch. 1 tr.) in sp. between next 2 groups of 3 tr. of previous round, rep. from * ending s.s. in 3rd of 4 ch.
3rd round—In D., 3 ch., 2 tr. in sp. between first and last groups of previous round, * 3 tr. in sp. between next 2 groups of 1 tr. 1 ch. 1 tr. of previous round, rep. from * ending s.s. in top of 3 ch.
4th round—In L., work s.s. into ch. sp. of last group of 1 tr. 1 ch. 1 tr. of 1 round below, 4 ch., 1 tr. in same ch. sp., * (1 tr. 1 ch. 1 tr.) in ch. sp. of next group of 1 round below, rep. from * ending s.s. in 3rd of 4 ch.
The last 2 rows form patt.
Work straight in patt. until Dress measures 10½ [12, 13½] in. (27 [30, 34] cm) from yoke line, ending with a 4th round.
** **Change to No. 9 hook**
Next round—In D., 1 ch., 1 d.c. in st. just worked into, * 1 d.c. in next ch. sp., 1 d.c. in each of next 2 tr., rep. from * ending 1 d.c. in last tr., join with s.s. in first ch.

Child's Dress and Hat

(continued)

Next round—In D., 1 ch., 1 d.c. in each d.c., ending s.s. in first ch.
Rep. last round twice ore.
Fasten off. **

SLEEVES

With No. 9 hook and D., make 31 [33, 35] ch., turn.
1st row—(Right side), 1 d.c. in 2nd ch. from hook, 1 d.c. in each ch. to end, turn with 1 ch. (30 [32, 34] sts.).
2nd row—1 d.c. in each d.c., turn with 1 ch.
Rep. last row twice more, turning with 3 ch. on last row.
Change to No. 8 hook
5th row—1 tr. in first d.c., * 1 tr. in next d.c., rep. from * to last d.c., 2 tr. in last d.c., turn with 3 ch. (32 [34, 36] sts.).
6th row—Miss first st., * 1 tr., in next tr., rep. from *, ending 1 tr. in top of 3 ch., turn.
Shape top as follows:—
7th row—s.s. over 4 sts., 3 ch., patt. to last 4 sts., turn.
8th row—s.s. over 1 st., 3 ch., patt. to last st., turn.
Rep. last row until 20 sts. remain.
Next row—s.s. over 2 sts., 3 ch., patt. to last 2 sts., turn.
Rep. last row once more (12 sts.).
Fasten off.

TO MAKE UP

With wrong side of work facing, press each piece lightly using a warm iron and slightly damp cloth.

Use a large tapestry needle and 12 in. (30 cm) lengths of yarn for make up, taking care the yarn remains twisted during make up.
Join right shoulder seam, then join left shoulder seam for ½ in. (1 cm) from side edge.
With right side facing for next row, No. 9 hook and D., work 4 rows d.c. all round neck.

BACK SHOULDER BORDER

With right side facing for first row, No. 9 hook and D., work 2 rows d.c. along back shoulder.
Fasten off.

FRONT SHOULDER BORDER

Work as for Back Shoulder Border with the addition of 3 buttonloops on last row.
First mark position of buttons on back shoulder with pins to ensure even spacing, then work buttonloops to correspond.
To make a buttonloop: 2 ch., miss 1 d.c.
Join sleeve seams.
Insert Sleeves with backstitch.
Press seams.
Sew on buttons to correspond with buttonloops.
Using 5 strands of yarn, make a chain and slot through row of trebles at underarm. Make and attach a pom-pon to each end of cord.

HAT

With No. 8 hook and D., make 4 ch., join in a ring with s.s.
1st round—3 ch., ino ring work 15 tr., join with s.s. in top of 3 ch. (16 sts.).
2nd round—3 ch., * 2 tr. in next st., 1 tr. in next st., rep. from * to last st., 2 tr. in last st., join with s.s. in top of 3 ch. (24 sts.).
3rd round—As 2nd round (36 sts.).
4th round—As 2nd round (54 sts.).
5th round—3 ch., 1 tr. in next st., 2 tr. in next st., * 1 tr. in each of next 2 sts., 2 tr. in next st., rep. from * ending s.s. in top of 3 ch. (72 sts.).
6th round—3 ch., 2 tr. in st. just worked into, * miss 2 sts., 3 tr. in next st., rep. from * ending miss 2 sts., s.s. in top of 3 ch. (24 groups of 3 tr.).
Join in L.
Work straight in patt. as for Skirt, starting with 2nd round, until Hat measures 6½ in. (17 cm), ending with a 4th round.
Work as for Skirt from ** to **
Press as for Dress.

(Paton's pattern)

Foreward and back entry

Any fabric using only a weft in production needs a form of binding to keep its shape. Shells of all kinds are used in crochet for many designs.

A welt or edging used in crochet is often called crochet moss stitch; stitches used chain and double crochet.

Where the forward and back entry are used, a rib can be obtained, in appearance like a knitted one. Mostly seen as a double rib, which will come out of shape with wear. If used as a single rib (see sample) this will be avoided, and it will retain shape after many washings.

It is not advisable, however, to use this rib on the front bands of a cardigan with buttons through. When one fabric lies on top of the other, it is very thick; the Moss stitch is more advisable.

In working front bands, work them in the same manner as knitting, stitching them on afterwards; this also ensures keeping better shape.

To work the forward entry. At the right side of the stitch, from the front, insert hook at the side of the upright threads, round the back, and out through the front, on the left side of the stitch. Draw yarn through here, and finish stitch as normal.

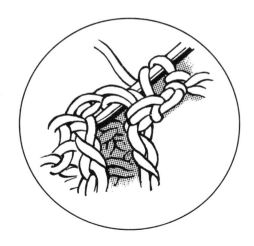

Fig. 23 *Back entry*

Fig. 22 *Forward entry*

Back entry is the same, working from the back of the work. Insert hook right side of stitch to the front, round and through on the left side of the stitch, out at the back, yarn being drawn through here, stitch worked as normal.

Items worked in the forward and backward entries produce a thick close fabric, using more yarns. Very worthwhile for both household and fashion. The pram cover further on uses the two entries and colour. If the same pattern was made in squares and sewn or crocheted together, a warm blanket or bedspread would result.

Combining these entries with others, further potential of the craft can be reached (see child's dress, and pancho).

Fig. 24 *Single Rib*
Ch 21 sts.
Entering the 3rd st, work 1 row in s-trs.
Pattern row. 3 ch for the turn and replacement of first st. * 1 tr fwd, 1 tr bk * ending 1 tr fwd.

Fig. 25 *Basket Stitch, only seen over 6 stitches, and 6 rows. Preferable in 4 stitches and 4 rows.*

Ch 25 sts, work 1 row in s-tr, starting at 3rd from hook.
1st row. 3 ch for the turn and first st, 1 tr bk, * 2 tr fwd, 2 tr bk *. Repeat * * to last 2 sts, 2 tr fwd.
2nd row. As first.
3rd row. 3 ch for the turn and first st, 1 tr fwd. * 2 tr bk, 2 tr fwd * ending with 2 tr bk.
4th row. As third row.

Pram cover in basket stitch

(see full colour illustration facing page 49)

Materials. 12 ounces of Sirdar Double Crepe in and 5 ounces in Contrast. Number 4.00(8) hook.
Tension. 4 stitches to 1 inch and 6 rows to 2 inches approximately.
Overall measurments. 21 inches by 31 inches.
With Contrast ch 72 sts, 1 tr into each from 4th.
Foundation row. 3 ch for the turn and first st, (this is on every row) 1 tr fwd * 2 tr bk 2 tr fwd. Repeat * *.
1st row. Drop contrast, do not break off join in main. 3 ch 1 tr fwd * 2 tr bk 2 tr fwd *. Repeat**
2nd row in main. 3 ch 1 tr bk, * 2 tr fwd 2 tr bk *. Repeat * *.
3rd row. Drop main and pick up contrast. 3 ch 1 tr bk * 2 tr fwd 2 tr bk *. Repeat * *.
4th row in contrast. 3 ch 1 tr fwd * 2 tr bk 2 tr fwd *. Repeat * *.
Continue in these four rows, till 70 rows (24 inches approximately) have been worked. Cast off. Sew in all ends.

OUTSIDE BAND IN MAIN

Starting at the exact corner point, 3 ch 1 tr, work across top in pattern, corner 2 tr 1 ch 2 tr, down side by working 1 tr into the first 2 rows, then 3 tr into every 2 rows, 5 sts to 4 rows, work corner, pattern along the bottom, adding an extra stitch at the beginning, to make up for the one worked along the side; work all round in this way.
The side flute will disappear when the proper pattern is worked on the following rows.
Work 8 rows in all basket stitch, working the extra stitches at the corners into the pattern.

FINAL BINDING ROW

Work dc in between each st. Cast off. Sew in end.

Man's boatnecked pullover

(see full colour illustration facing page 33)

Sizes

38 inch chest	28 ozs
40 inch chest	30 ozs
42 inch chest	32 ozs

Hayfield Croft Double Knitting Number 3.50 (9) and 3.00(10) Aero crochet hooks.

Tension. 5 sts to 1 inch—4 rows to 1 inch approximately.

See Abbreviations.

The main work is done up and down, the cuff and welt worked afterwards. All worked in short or half treble, the difference occurring with the entry.

Back. Using Number 3.50 hook.

Chain 67/69/71 loosely and evenly.

Work 1 s-tr into each st, starting at the 3rd ch from hook.

1st row. 3 ch for the turn, 1 s-tr into each st.

Raglan increase. Ch 5 sts, 1 s-tr in each st, at 3rd ch from hook.

Work 1 row in s-tr.

Repeat these 2 rows, 13/14/14 times in all.

Back Neck. Work straight for 22/22/26 rows. Last increase.

Raglan decrease starting at the bottom of the work. Work to within the last 3 sts, turn work back. Repeat till 64/66/68 sts remain, cast off end. Turn work to the bottom with right side facing you. Using No. 3.00, join in yarn and work 3 ch, into the bottom make, 75/79/85 s-tr.

The turn now replaces the first stitch.

1 s-tr fwd, - s-tr bk, entering round the upright threads. Repeat this last row till 2 inches. Cast off end. This is a single rib.

Front. Work as the back till 10/11/11 increases have been worked, ending at bottom.

As this is a round boat neck, the other decreases come in one side of the sleeve.

Neck decrease. Work to the last 2 sts, miss 1 st, work last st.

Make the ch turn, miss 1 st, work 2nd st.

Repeat last 2 rows, 3 times more and 1st once.

Work 14/14/18 rows.

Work twice into first st, next row, work twice into last st.

Repeat the last two rows, 3 times more and the 1st once.

Work Raglan decrease as back.

Complete as back.

Sleeves. These are worked the same, as the pattern is the same on each side. Still worked up and down as body of work, the decrease on the sleeve rather trying.

* Ch 13 sts, 1 s-tr into each st, starting at 3rd from hook making 11 working sts. ** Repeat ** making 22 working sts.

Raglan increase this side (as back) work rest of row.

Increase the 11 working sts at this wrist side. Continue increase each side till 92 sts.

Work straight across wrist edge, keeping raglan increase till 13/14/14 in all have been worked.

Work straight 4/6/8 rows, ending at wrist.

Next row, work to the last 2 sts, miss 1 st, work last.

Next row, turn, miss 1 st work from next.

Repeat the last 2 rows twice more.

Continue in raglan decrease as back, till 92 sts. You might find this very trying to reach.

Work to within the last 11 sts, turn work to within the last 3 sts, turn. Repeat till all sts are used up.

Using 3.00 hook, make a cuff of 41/43/45 sts.

Work 2 inches of rib, cast off.

To Make Up. Using backstitch, sloping through stepping stones, join 3 raglan seams.

Turn to the right side, with Number 3.00(10) hook.

Work 10/12/14 across sleeve, 34/34/38 across front, 10/12/14 across other sleeve, 24/24/28 sts across back. Work rib for 2 inches. As you work the neck will draw up.

Completion. Backstitch last remaining raglan and sleeve seams. Oversew side seams.

Top left: Disco Dress.
Top right: Dress with sleeves in long cross.
Left: Pancho using treble forward.

Left: Scarf, delicate in shell.
Left: Mans' boat necked pullover,
worked up and down.
Above: A casual jacket.

Fig. 26 *Treble Forward as in Pancho*

Ch 25 sts.

Foundation. Into 3rd ch, 2 tr * miss 1 st, tr into next st, miss 1 st 3 tr into next st. * Ending with 1 tr.

Pattern row. 3 ch and 2 tr into tr, * 1 tr fwd round 2nd of 3, into stem of single tr, 3 tr. * End row with 1 tr fwd.

Fig. 27 *Shell with back entry as Hooded Jacket*

Ch 27 sts.

Foundation row. 3 ch 3 tr into 3rd from hook, * miss 1 st, 1 tr, miss 1 st, 4 tr's into next *.

1st row. 3 ch, * between 2nd and 3rd tr, 4 tr, 1 tr bk round single tr *.

2nd row. 3 ch for turn, * between 2nd and 3rd tr- ltr, into stem of single tr- 4 tr, end by 1 tr into turn.

3rd row. 3 ch, * into 1 tr- ltr bk, between 2nd and 3rd tr 4 tr's working 1 tr into turn.

4th row. 3 ch, * into stem of tr- 4 tr, between 2nd and 3rd tr- ltr * ending with 4 tr.

Fig. 28 *Treble forward making feather pattern*

Ch 24 sts loosely.

Foundation row. 2 tr into 3rd st. * miss 1 st, 2 tr into next st ending row with 1 tr into last st.

1st row. 3 ch. * 1 tr fwd round first st of pair, 2 tr between this pair, 1 tr fwd round 2nd st of pr, miss next 2 sts. * Work 1 ch into turn.

2nd row. 3 ch, * 2 tr between 2nd and 3rd st of gr, 2 tr between grs * 1 tr into turn.

Three pointed Hat in traditional crochet

Materials: 1 ball each of main and contrast of Patons Promise.
Number 8 hook (400).

Sequence used 2 rounds main = 2 rounds contrast 4 rounds main = 3 times.

Special note: As this is worked in the round, the first tr is always replaced by 3 ch.
Turn work completely after each round to ensure perfect shape.
The block used for this design is 3 trebles.

Ch 6 sts, ss to form a ring.
Round 1. 1 blk 1 ch 6 times. ss to the 3rd ch to join. (Always join each round in this way).
Round 2. ss to the starting point on this round. Under first ch sp 1 blk 1 ch 1 blk, under next 1 blk, repeat twice more. You should now have a triangle which when laid flat will measure approxiately 2½ inches from corner ch sp.
Round 3-4-5-6. As second round, increasing on each by 1 blk at the sides.
For the next 8 rounds work only in single blks.
For the next 6 rounds, work as the first six, tracing down for the increases to fall in the same place and making 3 points again.
To finish. Work 1dc between the tr's of the blks, and 1dc under ch sp at the points. Cast off. Sew in ends. Turn up the points if required.

Cap and Berry

Materials for Cap: 2 balls of Patons Trident.

Materials for Berry: 1 ball of Patons Promise.

Number 8 (400) Crochet hook.

To fit the average head. If smaller size or larger size is required use a smaller or larger hook.

Tension. Approximately 4 single tr's to the inch.

Cap. ch 7 sts. ss to form a ring.

Round 1. Into this ring 3 ch (which always replaces first tr) 1 tr, * 1 ch 2 tr * 6 times in all 1 ch, making 7 ch sps. For next round, ss to third ch to join (always join in this manner).

Round 2. ss under ch sp. * Under this sp and each sp work gr (2 tr's 1 ch 2 tr's).

Round 3. * Under ch sp work gr, between gr's work 1 tr. * Repeat **.

Round 4. * Under ch sp work gr, each side of tr work 1 tr *. Repeat **. You have now increased 1 single tr between each point. Work as in round 4 till 9 single tr's have been worked.

Decrease round. * Work gr, miss first tr work 8 tr miss last *. Repeat **. Repeat last round 4 times more.

Band and peak. All worked in crochet moss st. 1 ch * 1 dc 1 ch * between each tr work as in the first rounds. 1 dc only under ch sp of gr.

Peak. Work 1 dc 1 ch 20 times, turn work back missing first place and working into next, forming decrease at the beginning of these 20 moss. Repeat last row 9 times more.

To complete. Work 1 dc into each st and ch. Sew on tassel or Pom Pom.

Berry. Work exactly as Cap, only working to 10 single tr's as this is worked in slightly finer yarn. Work band omit peak.

Blouse with Gilt Edging

(see illustration, frontispiece)

Materials: 9 [10, 10] balls (50 gram) Patons Promise.
No. 8 (4.00 mm) and No. 9 (3.50 mm) crochet hooks. 1 ball gold thread. Gold mesh belt.
Measurements: To fit bust 33-34 [35-36, 37-38] in. (84-86 [89-91, 94-96] cm).
Length from top of shoulders, 28 [28½, 29] in. (71 [72, 73] cm) excluding edging.
Sleeve seam, 2½ in. (6 cm) excluding edging, all sizes.

SIZES: The figures in square brackets [ ] refer to the 2 larger sizes.
Tension: 10 sts. to 2 in. (5 cm) in double crochet on No. 8 hook.
10 patt. rows = 2½ in. (6 cm).

BACK
** With No. 8 hook, make 106 [114, 122] ch.
Foundation row—1 d.c. in 2nd ch. from hook, 1 d.c. in each following ch., 105 [113, 121] sts. (in rows of d.c., starting ch. does not count as st.).
Work in patt. as follows:—
1st row—1 ch., 1 d.c. in each st., turn with 1 ch.
2nd to 5th row—As 1st row 4 times.
6th row—3 ch., 1 tr. in 1st st., * 1 ch., miss 3 sts., 3 tr. in next st. (1 group made), rep. from * to last 4 sts., 1 ch., miss 3 sts., 2 tr. in last st. (in lace pattern rows 3 ch. counts as 1st tr.).
7th row—3 ch., 1 tr. in 1st st., * 1 ch., 3 tr. in centre tr. of group, rep. from *, ending 2 tr. in top of 3 ch.
8th and 9th rows—As 7th row twice.
10th row—1 ch., 1 d.c. in each of next 2 sts., * 1 d.c. in next ch. sp., 1 d.c. in each of next 3 sts., rep. from *, ending last rep. 1 d.c. in top of 3 ch. These 10 rows form patt. Work rows 1 to 8 again.
Shape sides as follows:—
Next row—s.s. over 4 [5, 6] sts., patt. up to last turn. Keeping continuity of patt., dec. 1 st. as before at each end of every following 7th [7th, 6th] row until 89 [95, 101] sts. remain. Work straight until the 10 patt. rows have been worked 7 times in all and rows 1 to 8 again.

*** **Shape raglans** as follows:—
4 [5, 6] sts., turn. Keeping continuity of patt. dec. 1 st. at each end of next row, then on following alt. rows twice. Work 1 row straight (thus having completed the 5th patt. row). ** Now dec. 1 st. at each end of next 4 rows. Rep. last 10 rows once more (thus having completed the 9th patt. row), 53 [57, 61] sts. remain. *** Now continue in rows of d.c. only, decreasing 1 st. at each end of next and every alt. row until 31 [33, 35] sts. remain. Work 1 row straight. Fasten off.

FRONT
Work as for Back from ** to **, 75 [79, 83] sts.
3rd size only—Patt. 2 rows, decreasing 1 st. at each end of every row, (79 sts.).
All sizes—Divide for opening as follows:—
Next row—s.s. over 1st st., patt. 34 [36, 36], turn. Dec. 1 st. at raglan edge on next 3 [3, 1] rows, (thus ending with a 9th patt. row). Dec. 1 st at raglan edge on next row, then on following alt. rows twice. Work 1 row straight, then dec. 1 st. at raglan edge on next 4 rows (24 [26, 28] sts.). Now continue in rows of d.c. only, decreasing 1 st. at raglan edge on next and every alt. row until 18 [19, 20] sts. remain, ending with **wrong** side facing.
Shape neck as follows:—
Next row—s.s. over 3 [4, 5] sts., work to end. Continue decreasing 1 st. at raglan edge on next and every alt. row, and at the same time dec. 1 st. at neck edge on every row until 3 [3, 3] sts. remain, thus ending with a row on **wrong** side. Keep neck edge straight and work 1 more raglan dec. as before. Work 1 row straight. Fasten off. With right side facing, leaving centre 5 sts. unworked, rejoin yarn to next st. and patt. to last st., thus leaving last st. unworked. Finish to correspond with first side, reversing shapings.

SLEEVES
With No. 8 hook, make 58 [62, 66] ch. and work foundation row and 1st patt. row as for Back (57 [61, 65] sts.).

Next row—1 ch., 2 d.c. in 1st st., 1 d.c. in each following st. up to last st., 2 d.c. in last st. (59 [63, 67] sts.). Continue in patt. as for Back, shaping sides by decreasing 1 st. at each end of every alt. row until there are 65 [69, 73] sts., thus ending with an 8th patt. row.

Shape raglans as for Back from *** to *** when 29 [31, 33] sts. remain. Now continue in rows of d.c. only, decreasing 1 st. at each end of next and every alt. row until 7 sts. remain. Work 1 row straight. Fasten off.

TO MAKE UP

Press using a warm iron and slightly damp cloth. Join raglan seams.

Borders

Front and Neck: With No. 9 hook and right side facing, work 1 row d.c. up right side of front opening, round neck and down left side. Work 2 more rows d.c., working 3 d.c. in each corner. Break Promise, join in gold thread.

Picot edge—In gold thread, work 1 more row d.c. as before.

Next row—1 d.c. in 1st st., * 3 ch., 1 d.c. in same st. as last d.c. was worked into, 1 d.c. in each of next 2 sts., rep. from * to end. Fasten off.

Sleeves—With No. 9 hook, work 1 row d.c., then change to gold thread and work the 2 rows of picot edge.

Lower edges—Work back and front edges as for sleeve borders. Join side and sleeve seams. Neatly catch down sides of Front borders to unworked sts. of opening.

Belt loops—Make 2 lengths of ch. each 1½ in. (4 cm) long and attach to each side. Press seams as before.

(Paton's pattern)

Blouse with gilt edging

Pancho and Hat

(see full colour illustration facing page 32)

Materials: Robin Bri-Nylon Super Crimp Double Knitting 22 balls of main and 8 balls of contrast, ¾ ounces per ball. No. 3.50(9) Aero hook.

Tension: Approximately 4 sts to ¾ inches. Height and width of pattern ¾ inches.

Measurements: 30 inches down the centre point, 66 inches across.
Using stem and forward entry.
This pattern is worked to and fro after the first ring.
Back in main colour. 4 ch, ss to form ring.
Foundation. Into this ring 3 ch 4 tr's l ch 5 tr's turn. Commencing to work backwards and forwards along the rows.
1st row. 4 ch and 2 tr into first st, l tr forward into 3rd st, 3 tr into 5th st, l ch 3 tr into 6th st, l tr fwd into 8th, 3 tr into top of ch.
2nd row. Into first st, 4 ch 2 tr into 2nd st, l tr fwd 3 tr into stem of l tr, l tr fwd into 2nd of 3, centre, 3 tr l ch 3 tr under ch sp. l tr fwd into 2nd of 3, 3 tr into stem of single, l tr fwd into 2nd of 3, and 3 tr into last st.
3rd row and every row. 4 ch 2 tr in first st, l tr fwd into 2nd * 3 tr into stem of single, l tr fwd into 2nd of 3 * work centre under ch sp. Repeat ** working the last 3 tr into the top of turn.
Continue in this pattern for 9 inches from centre point. Change colour, 2 rows of contrast, 2 main, 2 contrast, 2 main, 2 contrast—10 main, 2 contrast, 2 main, 2 contrast, 6 main. Cast off.

Front. With main ch 51 sts.

Foundation. Into 3rd ch from hook, 2 tr * miss l, l tr into next, miss l 3 tr into next. * Repeat 4 times more, miss l st, l tr miss l st, 3 tr-l ch-3 tr into next miss l. Repeat **.

Work eight rows in main colour, change to contrast as back.
Sew the two sides together.
With contrast and from the right side, work l row round in pattern, turn work. Final edge 4 tr instead of 3 and l dc instead of tr. If you require fringe work 2 rows as pattern and add fringe.

Collar. Using main with right side to start, turning after each round.
3 ch to replace first st.
3 tr into seam, l tr into middle of square, 3 tr into raised st. Repeat to centre point, work 3 tr and place marker. Work pattern the other side join.
2nd round. Omit st on the centre 3 tr's.
3rd round. Work the 2 single tr's as a decrease at centre.
4th round. Decrease 3 single tr's at centre point.
5th round. Work centre point as 3 tr l ch 3 tr. Repeat 5th round 4 times more.
Finish off with the last two rows in contrast.

Hat to match Pancho, using 3 balls of main and 2 of contrast of same yarn and Number 3.50(9) hook.
Work as back in main till work measures 8 inches down centre point. (Work 5/6/7 inches instead of 8 inches if smaller size required.)
Straighten sides by working into first st, turn and l tr, pattern to centre, under ch 3 tr's, and work 2 tr into last sts.
2nd row. 3 ch for first st and turn pattern across to the other side, l tr into last st. Repeat these two rows, once more in main. 2 conrast 2 main, 2 contrast 2 main, 1 contrast and last as edge for pancho. Stitch the one seam, fold up top.

Hooded Jacket

(see full colour illustration facing page 17)

The Hooded Jacket is one of those designs where the 2 inch standard is not sufficient and needs a larger scale. The instructions are for 2 sizes. A suggested method of reaching the in-between sizes is to use one size smaller or larger crochet hook. This has been tried in other designs and proved very successful.

For size 33/34 inch bust 27 ounces of Hayfield Croft Double Knitting.

For size 38/39 inch bust 32 ounces of Hayfield Croft Double Knitting.

Number 4.00(8) hook. 6 buttons.

Tensions. Approximately 2 rows to 1 inch, 2 full patterns across 3 inches.

Back. Foundation ch 83/95 sts, 1 dc into 3rd from hook. * miss 1 st, 1 ch-1 dc into next *.

Welt row. (Crochet Moss Stitch). 2 ch, * 1 dc 1 ch into ch sp, * ending row 1 dc into last sp.

Pattern foundation row. 3 ch under 2nd ch sp, 4 tr. Miss 1 sp 1tr into next sp. * miss 1 st and sp, 4 tr into next st. Miss 1 sp and 1 dc, 1 tr into next sp *.

2nd foundation row. 3 ch, * between 2nd and 3rd tr-4 tr, 1 tr bk round single tr *.

1st pattern row. 3 ch and 1 tr in 1st tr, *between 2nd and 3rd tr- 1 tr, into stem of single tr, 4 tr * ending row with 2 tr into last st.

2nd pattern row. 3 ch 1 tr into 1st tr * 1 tr bk round single, 4 tr between 2nd and 3rd tr * ending row with 1 tr bk.

3rd row. 3 ch for first st and turn, * into stem of single tr, 4 tr between 2nd and 3rd tr- 1tr *

4th row, as 2nd foundation row.

These 4 rows form the pattern, repeat till work measures 18 inches.

Armhole decreases. ss over 1 full pattern, work to within 1 full pattern turn.

2nd decrease. ss over ½ pattern, work to within ½ pattern turn. Continue straight till work measures 7/8 inches.

Shoulder decrease. ss over 2 sh to single tr, work to within the same place other side. Cast off.

Right side. Ch 49/55 sts, and work as back welt.

Pattern. ss over 10 sts, into ch sp, 3 ch, miss next st and sp, * 4 tr into st, miss sp and st, 1 tr into next sp *.

Work as back decreasing one side for armhole till work measures 4/5 inches from first armhole decrease.

Neck decrease. Work both 1st and 2nd armhole decrease at the neck edge, continue straight as back, decrease for shoulder as back. Cast off.

Left side. As right, reversing all decreases. Back stitch shoulder seams on wrong side.

Hood. Starting on right side of work at the neck edge. Join in yarn, 3 ch and 1 tr, to shoulder work in 5 full pattern, work across back neck, (to obtain right length of jacket, there is one extra row out of pattern across here, which does not show in finished garment) down the other side to match.

Work in pattern for 10 inches, cast off yarn. Restart yarn at the beginning of the 5 centre patterns. Continue straight till work is the same length as sides when folded over. Cast off. Carefully oversew over 2 seams.

Bands. Join yarn on right side of work, at the 10 left stitches. Work in moss stitch for 5 inches from the bottom. Make button hole over 2 rows.

1st row. ch turn, 1 dc 1 ch into sp, 1 dc into next. Miss 1 sp, 3 ch 1 dc into next, 1 ch 1 dc into last.

2nd row. Work in moss stitch entering under the 3 ch sp twice. Work ten rows between button holes. (6 in all). Continue straight till work reaches the centre of hood when slightly stretched. Make the other side omitting button holes. Oversew to the sides by laying side by side.

Sleeves (making 2 alike). Ch 43/49 stitches, work as back for welt and first 6 rows.

Increase (over 4 rows).

1st row. Work 3 tr into first and last stitch.

2nd row. 4 tr into first and last stitch.

3rd row. 3 ch for turn, working pattern across row, and 1 tr into top of last sts.

4th row. 3 ch 1 tr into first st, 2 tr into last st. Work this 4 row increase 3 times in all, with 4 straight rows in between. Continue straight till work measures 17/17 inches.

Top decrease. Work the 1st armhole decrease, and 3 straight rows.

5th row. 1st decrease.

6th row. Straight.

7th row. As 5th.

8th row. Straight. Cast off. Oversew side seams of sleeves, and carefully backstitch into garment. Lightly press with a damp cloth and sew on buttons.

Sweater and Hat

Materials: Sleeveless Sweater: 2 [2, 2, 3] balls (50 gram) in A. 2 [2, 2, 2] balls (50 gram) in B., and 2 [2, 2, 2] balls (50 gram) in C. of Patons Double Knitting.
Number 4.00(8) hook.
Hat: 1 ball (50 gram) each in A., B. AND C. of Patons Double Knitting.
1 each crochet hooks 4.00 mm (8) and 5.00 mm (6).
Measurements: To fit 32 [34, 36, 38] in. bust.
Sleeveless Sweater: Length 19 [19, 19, 19] in.
Tension:
Sleeveless Sweater: 8 sts = 2 in. in width.
4 rows = 3 in. in depth.

SLEEVELESS SWEATER
FRONT
** Using 4.00 mm crochet hook and A., make 55 [59, 63, 67] ch.
Foundation row—1 d.tr. into 4th ch. from hook, 1 d.tr. into each ch. to end. Turn with 3 ch. (52 [56, 60, 64] sts.). Turning ch. not counted.
Next row—1 d.tr. into each st. to end. Break off A. Join in B. by drawing a ch. through loop on hook, work 2 ch., turn.
Continue in striped pattern.
1st row—Using B., 1 d.tr. into each st. to end. Turn with 3 ch.
2nd row—Using B., 1 d.tr. into each st. to end. Break off B. Join in C. by drawing a ch. through loop on hook, work 2 ch., turn.
3rd and 4th rows—Using C., work as 1st and 2nd rows, joining in A. at end of 4th row.
5th and 6th rows—Using A., work as 1st and 2nd rows, joining in B. at end of 6th row.
These 6 rows form pattern.
Inc. 1 st. at each end of next row, then every alt. row until there are 60 [64, 68, 72] sts.
Work 1 row.
Break off yarn, turn. **

Shape armholes and neck
Next row—Miss first 2 [3, 3, 4] sts., rejoin next colour into 3rd [4th, 4th, 5th] st. with a sl. st. and 3 ch., working again into the 3rd [4th, 4th, 5th] st., d.tr. 3 tog., 1 d.tr. into each of next 16 [16, 17, 17] sts., d.tr. 3 tog., turn with 3 ch.
Continue on these sts. as follows:—
D.tr. 3 tog. at each end of the next 3 rows.
Work 6 rows on remaining 6 [6, 7, 7] sts.
Fasten off.
Miss centre 12 [14, 16, 18] sts. for neck, rejoin yarn into the 13th [15th, 17th, 19th] st. with a sl. st. and 3 ch., working again into the 13th [15th 17th, 19th] st. d.tr. 3 tog. 1 d.tr. into each of next 16 [16, 17, 17] sts., d.tr. 3 tog. Turn with 3 ch. Now complete to match first side.

BACK
Work as for Front from ** to **.
Shape armholes
Next row—Miss first 2 [3, 3, 4] sts., rejoin next colour into 3rd [4th, 4th, 5th] st. with a sl.st. and 3 ch., working again into the 3rd [4th, 4th, 5th] st., d.tr. 3 tog., 1 d.tr. into each st. to the last 5 [6, 6, 7] sts., d.tr. 3 tog. Turn with 3 ch. D.tr. 3 tog. at each end of the next 3 rows.
Work 4 rows on the remaining 40 [42, 46, 48] sts.
Shape neck
Next row—1 d.tr. into each of first 7 [7, 8, 8] sts., d.tr. 3 tog. Turn with 3 ch.
Next row—D.tr. 3 tog., 1 d.tr. into each st. to end.
Fasten off.
Miss centre 20 [22, 24, 26] sts. for neck, rejoin yarn into the 21st [23rd, 25th, 27th] st. with a sl.st. and 3 ch., working again into the 21st [23rd, 25th, 27th] st., d.tr. 3 tog., 1 d.tr. into each st. to end.
Turn with 3 ch.
Next row—1 d.tr. into each st. to last 3 sts., d.tr. 3 tog.
Fasten off.

Sweater and Hat

Continued

MAKE UP
Press each piece lightly with warm iron and damp cloth. Sew shoulder and side seams.

NECK BORDER
Join A. yarn to back neck edge at right shoulder and work a row of firm d.c. all round neck edge, working 1 d.c. for each st. or 3 d.c. for each row. Join with a sl.st. Turn with 2 ch.
Next row—Miss sl.st., 1 tr. into each st. to end. Join with a sl.st. Turn with 2 ch. Rep. last row once more. Join with a sl.st.
Fasten off.

ARMHOLE BORDERS
Join A. yarn at side seam, and work a row of d.c. all round armhole edge, working 1 d.c. for each st., or 3 d.c. for each row. Join with a sl.st. Turn with 1 ch.
Next row—1 d.c. into each of first 16 sts., 1 tr. into each st. to the last 16 sts., 1 d.c. into each of last 16 sts. Join with a sl.st. Turn with 1 ch.
Following row—1 d.c. into each of first 10 sts., 1 tr. into each st. to last 10 sts., 1 d.c. into each of last 10 sts. Join with as l.st.
Fasten off.
Press seams and borders lightly.

HAT
Using 5.00 mm crochet hook and A., make 6 ch. and join with a sl.st. to form a ring.

1st round—2 ch., 17 tr. into ring. Join with a sl.st. into 2nd of 2 ch.
2nd round—2 ch., 2 tr. into each tr. to end. Join with a sl.st. into 2nd of 2 ch. Break off A.
3rd round—Join in B., by drawing a ch. through loop on hook, 1 ch., * 2 tr. into next tr., 1 tr. into following tr., rep. from * to end. Join with a sl.st. into 2nd of 2 ch.
4th round—2 ch., 1 tr. into each tr. to end. Join as before. Break off B.
5th round—Join in C. by drawing a ch. through loop on hook, 1 ch., * 2 tr. into next tr., 1 tr. into each of following 2 tr., rep. from * to end. Join as before.
6th round—As 4th round. Join as before. Break off C.
Continue in stripes of 2 rows in each colour and work 6 rounds in tr. as 4th round. Break off C.
Change to 4.00 mm crochet hook, join in A. and work 4 rounds of d.c.
Change to 5.00 mm crochet hook.
Next round—1 ch., * 2 tr. into next st., 1 tr. into following st., rep. from * to end. Join with a sl.st. into 1 ch. Break off A.
Now work 6 rounds of tr., changing colour as before, then work 2 more rounds in A. Fasten off.

MAKE UP
Fold last 2 rows to wrong side and sl.st. neatly. Sew in ends. Press lightly.

(Paton's pattern)

44

A Shimmering Sweater

To fit bust					
	in.	31-32	33-34	36-37	38-39
	cm	79-81	84-86	91-94	96-99

Patons Promise
✕50 gram balls   7   7   8   8

No. 9 (3.50mm) and No. 8 (4.00mm) crochet hooks. 3 buttons.

Tension
12 sts. and 7½ rows to 2in. (5 cm) over patt. on No. 8 hook.

BACK
With No. 9 hook, make 87/92/102/107 ch.

Foundation row—(Right side), 1 d.c. in 2nd ch. from hook, 1 d.c. in each ch. to end, turn (86 [91, 101, 106] d.c.).

Next row—1 d.c. in first d.c., 1 d.c. in each d.c. to end, turn.
Work 1 row more in d.c.

Next row—1 d.c. in first 3 [5, 5, 2] d.c., (2 d.c. in next d.c., 1 d.c. in each of next 7 [7, 8, 9] d.c.) 10 times, 2 d.c. in next d.c., 1 d.c. in each d.c. to end, turn (97 [102, 112, 117] sts.).

Change to No. 8 hook and patt. as follows:—
1st row—5 ch., miss first st., * y.o.h., draw loop through next st., y.o.h., draw loop through 2 loops on hook, (miss next st., y.o.h., draw loop through next st., y.o.h., draw loop through 2 loops on hook) twice, y.o.h., draw loop through all 4 loops on hook, 4 ch., rep. from * to last st., ending last rep. with 2 ch. in place of 4 ch., 1 tr. in last st., turn.

2nd row—3 d.c. in first 2 ch. sp., * 5 d.c. in next 4 ch. sp., rep. from * to last 5 ch. sp., 3 d.c. in 5 ch. sp., 1 d.c. in 3rd of 5 ch., turn.

3rd row—1 d.c. in first d.c., * 1 d.c. in each d.c., to end, turn.
These 3 rows form patt.
Work straight in patt. until Back measures approx. 14 in. (36 cm), ending with a 3rd patt. row.

Shape armholes as follows:—

1st row—s.s. across 5 sts., patt. to last 5 sts., turn.

2nd and 3rd rows—In patt.
Rep. 1st to 3rd row 2 [2, 3, 3] times (67 [72, 72, 77] sts.). **
Work straight until Back measures 21 [21, 21½, 22] in. (53 [53, 54, 56] cm), ending with a 2nd or 3rd patt. row. Fasten off.

FRONT
Work as Back to ** (67 [72, 72, 77] sts.).
Work straight until Front measures approx. 18 [18, 18, 18½] in. (46 [46, 46, 47] cm), ending with a 3rd patt. row.

Shape neck

Next row—Patt. 27 [27, 27, 32], turn.

Next 2 rows—In patt.

Next row—s.s. across 5 sts., patt. to end, turn.

Next 2 rows—In patt.

Next row—Patt. 17 [17, 17, 22], turn.
Work straight until Front matches Back at armhole edge. Fasten off.
Leaving centre 13 [18, 18, 13] sts. free, rejoin yarn to next st., patt. to end, turn.

Next 2 rows—In patt.

Next row—Patt. 22 [22, 22, 27], turn.

Next 2 rows—In patt.

Next row—s.s. across 5 sts., patt. to end, turn (17 [17, 17, 22] sts.).
Complete to match first half.

A Shimmering Sweater

Continued

SLEEVES

With No. 9 hook, make 55 [55, 59, 63] ch. and work Foundation row as on Back (54 [54, 58, 62] d.c.).

Work 10 [10, 4, 4] rows more in d.c.

Next row—1 d.c. in first 1 [1, 2, 2] d.c., (2 d.c. in next d.c., 1 d.c. in each of next 2 d.c.) 17 [17, 18, 19] times, 2 d.c. in next d.c., 1 d.c. in last 1 [1, 1, 2] d.c., turn (72 [72, 77, 82] sts.).

Change to No. 8 hook and work in patt. as on Back until sleeve seam measures approx. 4½ in. (11 cm), ending with a 3rd patt. row.

Shape top by working 1st to 3rd row of armhole shaping as on Back 5 [5, 5, 6] times (22 [22, 27, 22] sts.). Fasten off.

TO MAKE UP AND NECK BORDER

Press using a warm iron and slightly damp cloth.

Join right shoulder, then join left shoulder for 1 inch (2 cm).

Join side and sleeve seams and insert Sleeves.

With right side facing for 1st row and No. 10 hook, work 2 rows in d.c. all round neck.

Fasten off.

With **wrong** side facing, rejoin yarn and work 1 row more.

Fasten off.

Make 3 buttonloops on left front shoulder.

Sew on buttons to correspond.

Press seams.

(Paton's pattern)

Arm bag

(see full colour illustration facing page 16)

Materials: 2 and 3 row under entry. Made with 4 ounces of main and 3 ounces of contrast.

Using a Number .00(8) hook.

With main yarn ch 57 sts, and work 1 dc from 2nd along the row.

1st row. 1 ch and 1 dc into 1st st. * miss 3 sts-3 ch 1 dc into next *.

2nd row. 1 ch 1 dc into 1st dc, * 3 ch 1 dc into previous dc *.

Change to contrast yarn, do not break off main, whichever side the yarn is left, any row can be worked from.

3rd row. 1 ch 1 dc into 1st dc, * into 2nd of the missed sts on the 3rd row, 1 tr, pulling the loop to level of the row, under the 2 ch's 1 tr, and into the 2nd miss st 1 tr, (forming a shell), 1 dc into previous dc. These 3 rows from the pattern. Continue till pattern has been made 10 times in all. ss to 3rd dc, work to within 3rd dc turn, complete pattern on these stitches.

2nd decrease. ss to the 2nd dc, work to within the last 2 dc's, turn, complete pattern on these sts. Repeat the last decrease till the pattern makes 2 shells. Work another 3 full patterns. Cast off. Turn work, across the bottom work 10 rows of dc's, working the first over the first row of finished side. Complete as other side, and join top by dc together.

Join the sides from the bottom by working 9 shells to the opening, 1 dc into 1st place, 1 dc-1 tr-1dc into next. Round top work 36 dc's to the top and 36 dc's to the join. Turn. Work another row in dc, decreasing over 2 sts, every 6th and 7th st. Work 2 more rows in dc on the sts left, and a finishing row of shells, (1 dc, miss 1 st, 1dc-1tr-1dc into next, miss 1 st).

Add fringe of 4 strands, cutting first lengths 12 inches, trim when complete. Add the extra on the finished bag as shown in picture.

Cover ups. *Left:* Lace pattern. *Right:* Grandmas' traditional crochet.

Cushion cover using back loops.

Cushion cover using back loop, making ridged squares.

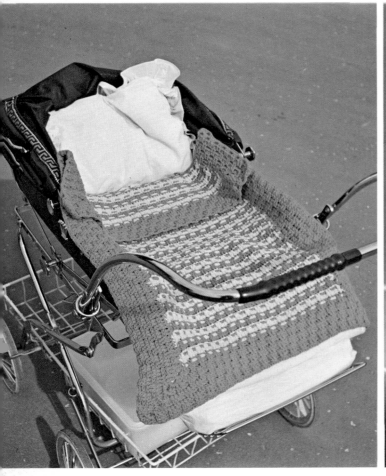

Pram cover using basket stitch.

Pharoah's hat and scull cap, so much like knitting

Shawl in King Solomon's Knot

King Solomon's Knot, the oldest of all crochet stitches, being made in only double crochet and chain. (See picture of shawl). The chain is made with a difference and called long chain. Before you form the stitch, the loop on the hook is pulled up to the length required, then stitch is completed, which will vary according to the type of yarn used. Finer yarn small pull, thicker yarns longer pull. Try a small sample.

1 ch * 1 long ch (pulled $\frac{1}{2}$ inch), into the back thread of this, 1 dc (knot). * Repeat 14 times in all.

Foundation. 1 long chain, slip hook through back loop, 1 dc each side of 4th dc (when working the first, draw yarn through the 3 loops on hook).
* 1 long ch-lk-1 long ch, slip hook back thread, miss lk, 1 dc each side of next k. * Repeat ** ending by working 1 dc into the last knot and not at the side. On the first row, you will enter under 1 top thread.

2nd row. * 1 long ch-lk-1 long ch, slip hook, 1dc each side of single k. * (the entry will now be under 2 threads). Repeat ** working last as before.

Shawl

Materials: 9 balls of Hayfield Brig Aran Type Yarn. No. 5.00(6) crochet hook.
Width across top approximately 86 inches.
Length at the centre point down approximately 40 inches.

Tensions. Long ch and k approximately 1 inch. Method of joining yarn splicing.

Foundation. Work 1 ch, * 1 long ch ($\frac{3}{4}$ inch) 1 dc into its back thread. Repeat 108 times in all.
2nd row. 1 ch, slip hook through back thread, 1 dc each side of 3rd k from hook. * 1 long ch-lk-1 long ch, slip hook, miss 1 k, 1dc each side of next k * Repeat ** to last 2 k's, miss 1, 1 dc into the last k. After this row, the entry will be under 2 threads.
3rd and every row, forming a decrease each end. 1 long ch, slip hook, 1 dc into first k. * 1 long ch-1dc-1 long ch, miss k of 3, 1 dc each side of single k. * Repeat * to the last k. 1 dc only into this. Repeat third row till no stitches are left.

Edging. Starting at the straight piece along the top. 1 dc into each k, with 2 ch between (ordinary ch). Down to the point and back, 5 ch, ss to 3rd, 2 ch, 1 dc into k.
If required a fringe or tassels may be added, which will use a great deal of yarn.

"Solomon's Knot, a tie of three
Secure as the Blessed Trinity"

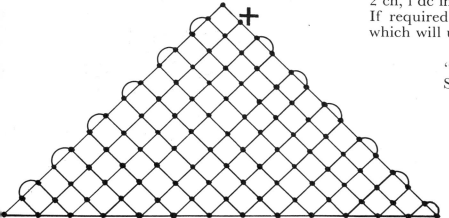

Fig. 29 *Diagram of shawl in miniature*

(The loops at the side represent 1 long ch. The X where work finally ends.)

Child's dress and boy's sweater

(see full colour illustration facing page 16)   **Child's Dress to fit 3 or 5 year old**

Materials: Hayfield Bri-Nylon Super Crimp Double Knit in ¾ ounce balls.

3 years (18)   12 balls
5 years (20)   14 balls
Number 3.00(10) and .00(8) Aero crochet hooks.

Tensions.

Yoke   4 trebles to 1 inch approximately.
          5 rows to 1 inch approximately.
Skirt   4 sts to 1 inch approximately.
          8 rows to 3 inches approximately.

The skirt of this dress is a continuation of the feather pattern, taken over 4 rows, reversing the groups on the third.

Back working from the waist to shoulder.

With Number 3.00 hook ch 50/56 sts. Work 6/8 rows in tr, starting at 4th from hook. First st is the turn, from second row entering stem.

Armhole decreases. ss over 5/7 sts. Work to within 5/7 sts turn. Continue straight 6/7 inches from beginning, cast off. Turn work to start the skirt from waist down.

Foundation. Join yarn at the end, ch 3 sts, into next 2 sts work gr * (Group 1 tr fwd round 1st st, 2 tr's between the 2 sts, 1 tr fwd round 2nd st), miss 1 st * Repeat ** working 1 tr at the end.

1st pattern row. 3 ch for the turn, * 2 tr between 2nd and 3rd st of gr, 2 tr between the gr * Repeat ** ending with 1 tr on top of ch turn.

2nd pattern row. 3 ch for turn. * miss first 2 tr's, work gr over next 2 tr's * Repeat ** ending row with 1 tr on top of turn.

3rd row. As first, working in reverse.

4th row. 3 ch for turn, * 1 gr into 1st 2 tr's, miss 2 tr's * Repeat, ending row with fwd gr and 1 tr. Repeat till skirt measures 11½/13½ inches. Cast off.

Front. Work as back till work measures 4/5 inches.

Neck division. Work across 9/11 sts turn. Work as back on these. Work the other side on the last 9/11 sts to match. Turn and make skirt, as back.

Sleeves. With a Number 3.00 hook ch 38/44 sts. Work as yoke for 5/6 inches, change to No. 4.00 hook. Work pattern for a further 5/6 inches. Cast off.

To Make Up. Sew seams of dress and work 1 finishing row round the bottom. 1 dc into each st of gr, 1 dc between 2 tr's 1 row down. Work 1 row of trebles round the neck, 6/7 sts down the side of neck. Round this work a simple shell of 5 tr's into 1st place, 1 dc into 2nd.

Make a ch of 36 inches, thread through waist add tassels.

Sew the sleeves to the last 3 rows of tr's, set squarely into armhole and sew.

Work a finishing row round the bottom of sleeve.

ONE ROW DOWN ENTRY

One row down entry, usually making a close fabric, very suitable for male garments.

To try it first ch 24 sts. Starting at 2nd ch from hook, 1 dc * miss 1 st, 1 dc into next * Repeat **.

1st row. 1 ch for turn only. * Into 1st st 1 dc, 1 tr into st under ch sp, 1 row down * ending with 1 dc.

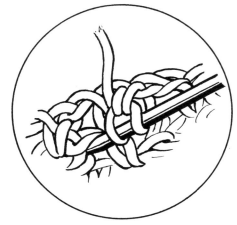

Fig. 30 *One row down entry*

Child's dress and boy's sweater
Continued

2nd row. l ch for turn. Into first st l dc, * miss l st l dc into next * Repeat **.

SMALL BOY'S SWEATER IN 3 SIZES

Materials: Hayfield Beaulon 4 ply fingering.

26 inch chest	10 ounces
28 inch chest	11 ounces
30 inch chest	12 ounces

Number 3.00(10) Aero hook.

Tensions. 5 stitches to 1 inch approximately. 5 full patterns to 2 inches approximately.

Back. Ch 64/70/76 sts.

Foundation row. Worked in s-tr, starting at 3rd from hook. Single rib.
3 ch for turn and 1st st. * l tr fwd l tr bk.
Make rib for 2½ inches. Change to pattern.

1st row. l ch for turn throughout. (It does not replace 1st st in pattern). Into 1st st l dc, * miss l st, l ch l dc into next *. Repeat **.

2nd row. Into 1st st l dc, * into st below ch sp, one row down work l tr, into next st l dc *. Repeat **. These 2 rows from the pattern. Continue straight till the work measures 10½/11½/12½ inches.

Armhole decreasing. ss over to 3rd dc, work to within the 3rd dc from end, turn.

2nd decrease over 3 sts. After l ch turn, work dc till 2 loops on hook, work tr till 3 loops on hook, work next dc till 4 loops on hook, yarn round hook draw through all 4 loops, work this decrease the same at the other end of row. Work one row and repeat 2nd decrease row once more. Continue straight to 16/17½/19 inches.

Shoulder decrease. Work as 1st armhole decrease. Work 1 row. Repeat once more.

Neck band. ss over to 3rd dc, work s-tr into each st, to within the 3rd dc from end, turn. Work 3 rows in single rib. Cast off.

Front. Work as back to armhole decrease. Place small safety pin in the exact centre of work. Make the armhole decrease at the beginning of the row, work to the dc at the side of the centre tr, turn work back.
After the first pattern row has been worked, decrease 3 sts at the neck edge. Keeping the side straight, decrease on the 6th row and 12th row neck edge, then 16th and 20th. Work straight as back, decrease shoulder. Cast off. Starting at the dc the other side of the pin, make the second side to match, reversing all decreasings.

Neck band. Work 30 s-tr down to the pin at centre, l st into centre. 30 sts, up the other side. 3 rows of single rib, decreasings over 3 sts at centre point.

Sleeve (2 alike). Ch 34/38/42 sts.
Work in single rib for 2½ inches. Change to pattern for 4 rows. Increase on the next and every 4th row by working twice into 1st and last stitch till 53/57/61 sts. Work all extra sts in dc's till you have enough for pattern. Continue straight till 11/13½/15 inches.

Armhole decreasings. Work 1st armhole decrease and 2nd pattern row. Work 4/6/8 row of pattern. Decrease over 3 sts at each end of next alternate rows, (this is one time when the alternate decrease can be used in crochet) 4/5/6 times, cast off.

Finish off. Backstitch shoulder seams, and sleeves into garment. Oversew all other seams. Lightly press with a dry cloth, NOT THE RIB.

Long cross and how to make it

Ch 24 sts.

y.r.h. twice, enter 5th st from hook, d.y.t., * y.r.h. once, d.y.t. 2 loops (3 loops on the hook), miss 1 st, y.r.h. d.y.t. next st, (y.r.h. draw through 2 lps, repeat till 1 lp), make 1 ch, 1 tr into the 2 centre loops of cross. Repeat cross over 3 sts to the end of row, working 1 ltr into last st.

Pattern row. 4 ch for the turn, make a cross entering the stems at the top of the cross, and working 1 ltr into last st.

Working the crosses exactly the same, enter under the ch sp. At the end of the row, finished last cross, working between previous and ch turn. Work 1 ltr into ch turn.

See the difference in the finished fabric, when the entry is altered. The cross can be wide as seen in the waistcoat and bag, or can be narrow as seen in the sleeves of the dress.

Fig. 31 *Long Cross*

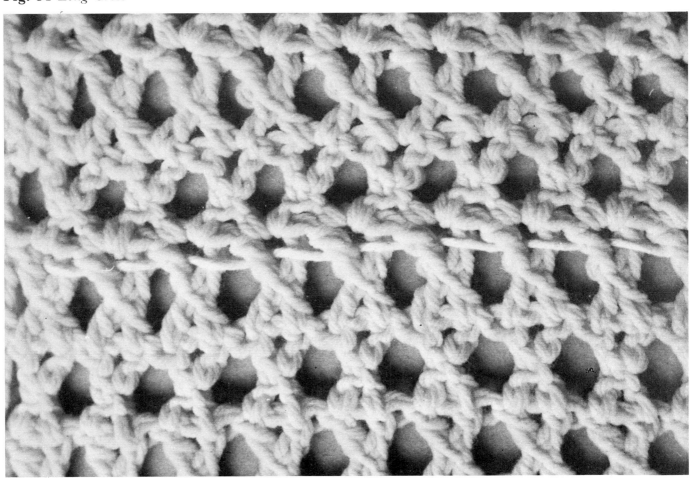

Waistcoat and Shoulder bag

(see full colour illustration facing page 65)

WAISTCOAT IN THREE SIZES

Materials: Lavenda Double Knitting

Size 32 bust	9 ounces main	3 contrast
Size 35 bust	10 ounces main	3 contrast
Size 38 bust	11 ounces main	4 contrast

Number 3.00(10) Aero hook.

Tensions. 5 double crochet to 1 inch approximately. 1 pattern to 1 inch approximately.

Back. Ch 82/90/98 sts. l dc into each st from 2nd.

1st pattern row. Ch 4 sts (which is the turn). y.r.h. twice, enter first st, d.y.t., y.r.h. draw through 2 loops (leaving 3 on hook) miss 2 sts, y.r.h. enter next st d.y.t. (5 lps) work of as in l tr till 1 loop. 2 ch l tr into 2 lps at the centre. Cross formed. Repeat along the row over 4 sts, working 1 ltr into last st.

2nd pattern row. l ch turn only * into l tr, ldc, into stem first bar, ldc, into ch, 2 dc's, into stem 2nd bar l dc. * Repeat **. These 2 rows form the pattern. Work straight till work measures 18 inches.

Armhole decreases. ss over 2 cross, work to within 2 cross, turn. ss over 1 cross work to within 1 cross. Straight till work measures 7/7/8 inches from first decrease, cast off.

Sew in end.

Left side. Ch 38/46/52 sts.

Work as back till work measures 16 inches.

Front decrease. Work to the last cross omit the 2 ch and tr.

2nd row. Miss 1st st start row at second. Remembering to work the armhole decreases after 18 inches at the other side, work the front decrease on the next 3rd and 6th pattern. Continue straight till length of back, cast off.

Right front. As left reversing the decreasing. Omitting the part of the cross is the same for each side. Join waistcoat together by crocheting in dc's on wrong side.

Front band. Starting at the right side of work from back shoulder, work dc's across back, down sides work ldc into dc row, and 3 dc's under long st., twice into each corner Across bottom, l dc into 3 sts miss l st and the other side to match ss to join. Work 3 more rounds of dc's turning work after each round.

Arm bands. Join yarn under arm seam, work 75/75/83 sts and 3 row of dc's, turning work after each round.

Fold yarn into 12 inch lengths, cut and use in two's for a fringe all round the bottom.

SHOULDER BAG

Materials: 4 ounces of Lavenda Double Knitting in Dark and 1 ounce in Light.

Number 4.00(8) hook.

Tensions. Approximately, 2 tr's rounds to 1 inch, 1 C to 1 inch.

Width across centre without fringe 13 inches.

The 3 ch at the beginning at each round represents the first stitch. Entry between sts for tr's. In dark yarn ch 4 sts, ss to join ring. (ss to join in each round).

Round 1. 18 tr's.

Round 2. In Light. 3 ch into next sp ltr, 5 ch and ltr into join of ch and first tr, making first C. * Make Cr's over 2 sps at the bottom with 2 ch between top bar. (9 Cr's).

3rd round (with dark yarn). Into stem of cr's l tr, under ch 2 tr's, into stem of last bar l tr *.

4th round (in dark). * l tr into first sp, 2 tr's into next sp *.

5th round (with light). As 2nd, making 18 cr's.

6th round as 3rd.

7th round. * l tr into 2 sps, 2 tr into 3rd sp *.

8th round. As 2nd making 36 cr's.

9th round. As 3rd.

10th round. To straighten Top, 5 ch into next sp, t tr, into next 3 sps, l l tr, into next 16 sps, l tr, into next 3 sps, l l tr, into next 2 sps, t tr, make l ch, into next 2 sps, l tr tr, into next 3 sps, l l tr, and l tr in each sp to within 5. 3 l tr, 2 tr tr. Make another side exactly the same. Join together in dc's going through 2 sides. Do not break yarn.

Handle and finish. ch 130 sts, l dc into the other seam, working in dc's all the time, dec first 2 sts, work to within the last 2 sts of top, dec. Dec 2 sts on the handle, work round and dec in the same manner on the opposite side. Work 2 more rows in this way with the decreases. Repeat on the other side of top and handle, fold handle and join by working dc's through the two sides. Sew in end, Line and add Fringe starting with 2 strands cut in 12 inch lengths when folded. When complete lay flat, trim as desired.

Pelerine

(see full colour illustration facing page 64)

Materials. Using Hayfield Gaylon Double Knitting.

Bust Size	Oyster (Main)	Pink	Yellow	Purple
34 inches	14	3	4	3
36 inches	16	3	5	3
38 inches	18	4	7	4

Size 350 (Number 9) Crochet hook. 3 buttons.

SPECIAL NOTE

This garment is worked in one piece in the round, which must be turned after every round (slip stitch to next starting place) to obtain perfect shape, and the sun-ray effect. The first stitch is replaced by 3 ch and each entry is into the STEM and not standard.

If a smaller size is required, allow 4 inches more than the normal bust size, adjusting materials with the help of the chart. Smaller the round less yarn larger a lot more if made for 40 bust.

Best method of joining yarn when working round is splicing.

Sew in ends as you go along, this enable them to be worked over.

Centre. With yellow yarn, ch 4 sts, ss to join and form ring.

1st round. 16 tr's into this ring (remembering 3 ch replaces first st). Break off yellow, turn work.

2nd round in Purple. In between each st, work 2 tr's, breakk off purple.

3rd round in Pink. * Between 2 tr's of previous round, work 2 tr's, over next 2 tr's dec *. (After

dec has been worked, it is ignored and the next dec stitches used are each side of this). Repeat**.

4th round in Pink. As 3rd.

5th round in Purple. As 3rd.

6th round in Yellow. * Between 2 tr's, work 4 trs, dec over 2 tr's *. Repeat **.

7th round in Yellow. * Between 2nd and 3rd st of 4 tr's, work 2 tr's, l tr into 3rd st, dec over 2, l tr into 2nd st of next 4 *. Repeat **.

Pattern in Main

1st round. * Between 2 trs, work 2 trs, l tr into next st, dec over 2 sts, l tr into next st *. Repeat **.

2nd round. * Between 2 trs, work 4 trs, l tr into next st, dec over 2 sts, l tr into next st *. Repeat **. Continue in pattern, working the extra stitches gained in round, in treble, till work measures, 38/40/42 inches, when laid flat, across from Increase to Decrease. (This is the measuring point if smaller or even larger size is required).

Border. Worked in centre colours. Still keeping to pattern work rounds 2 Yellow, 1 Purple, 2 Pink, 1 Purple.

Next round in yellow, making buttonholes.

Work to first decrease, miss the 2 sts, work 7/8/9 sts, miss 1 st, work l ch, l tr into next 7/8/9 sts, miss 1 st, work as pattern round from next st.

Next round in Yellow. Work in pattern all round, working l tr into the l ch of previous row. Finally, work 1 round in dc to bind edge.

To complete: Lightly press with a damp cloth. From the first buttonhole at the decrease point, press back 4 scallops, this forms your collar. Sew on buttons.

Dress

(see full colour illustration facing page 32)

Materials: Sirdar Courtelle Crepe.
25 balls for size 12 length centre back 34 inches.
27 balls for size 14 length centre back 34½ inches.
29 balls for size 16 length centre back 35 inches.
If longer length is required, allow 1 ball extra for every 1½ inches size 12, a little more for larger sizes. Number 3.00(10) Aero hook.

Tensions. 4 tr sts to 1 inch approximately.
5 rows to 2 inches approximately.
The cross row on sleeves and collar ¾ inch approximately.

Note. All treble entry into the stem throughout.

Back. Ch 90/94/98 sts.

Foundation row. 1 tr into each st starting at the 4th from hook. Making 88/92/96 working sts.

1st row and every row. 3 ch for the turn and first st, 1 tr into each st.

Work straight for 14 inches. As fashion cannot make up its mind where to place the hem line, at this point it can be done. If mini is required, work 8 or 10 inches, before decrease, depending on how short you require your mini. Also add the extra length at this point to maxi or midi.

Hip decrease. Work 2 clear rows between each dec. Dec over 2 sts making 1 dec over 3 sts making 1. The number are worked in tr's.

1st dec row. 1-dec2-22/23/24-dec3-32/34/36-dec3-22/23/24-dec2-1.

2nd dec row. 1-dec2-20/21/22-dec3-30/32/34-dec3-20/21/22-dec2-1.

3rd dec row. 1-dec2-18/19/20-dec3-28/30/32-dec3-18/19/20-dec2-1.

4th dec row. 1-dec2-16/17/18-dec3-26/28/30-dec3-16/17/18-dec2-1.

5th dec row. 1-dec2-14/15/16-dec3-24/26/28-dec3-14/15/16-dec3-1.

Work 8 straight rows.

Bust increase
1st inc. 16/17/18-inc-24/26/28-inc-16/17/18.
Work 2 rows.
2nd inc. 17/18/19-inc-26/28/30-inc-17/18/19.
3rd inc. 18/19/20-inc-28/30/32-inc-18/19/20.
4 rows straight.

Armhole decrease. ss over to 7th/8th/9th st work across to within 6th 7th 8th st turn. Continue straight to 7/7½/8 inches, cast off.

Front. As back to 5½/6/6½ inches after armhole decrease. Work across 16/17/18 sts, for one side, work as long as back, cast off.
Work the last 16/17/18 sts in the same manner.

Backstitch side seams, sloping at the end, over the straight piece. Oversew shoulder seams.

Finish off bottom working, * ldc into 2 sts, ldc 3 ch ldc into next *.

Collar. Turn work to right side join on yarn at shoulder seam. First c, 3 ch, miss 1 st 1 tr into next, 4 ch, 1 tr into join of ch and first sts. Continue in c's over each 3 sts of back, 1 c on every row down side, across front over 3 sts, up the other side on each row, ss to 3rd ch. Turn work, now and after every round. ss to first ch sp, make first c from here and under next ch sp, as seen in the sample. Work 6 rounds of c's in all, finish by working ldc 3 ch lds under each ch sp.

Sleeves making 2 alike.
Ch 56/60/64 sts, not tight.

Foundation row. Make c over 3 sts, starting at 5th from hook. 1 st is missed between the bottom bars, and 1 ch worked between the top bars. Repeat along the row, 1 ltr into last st.

2nd row. 4 ch for turn and first st. Make Crs, entering under 1st and 2nd ch sp, next c 2nd and 3rd sp, repeat along the row. Into the last c, 1 bar under sp, 2nd bar between c and last st, 1 L tr into last st.

Pattern row with increase.
Each row will increase by 2 cr's. ½ on each side section and full on centre on section. Work 5/5/6 c's make 2nd bar entry, between c's. Next C, 1st bar into last place, 2nd bar under following ch sp. Work 5/6/5 c's Inc, work 5/5/6 c's. Repeat this row till 17 inches measured down centre. After the first few rows, you will notice the hole will be bigger where the inc falls, which helps as a guide.

Cuff. 3 ch for turn, under 1st and 2nd sp, work a 2 tr dec. Repeat in every 2 sps along row, ending with 1 tr into last st.
This has now drawn work together.
Work 5 inches in tr's.
Finish off with a ch lp edging by working, 1 dc into first 2 sts, ldc 3 ch 1 dc into next st.
Oversew together the seams to the last 2 c's, set squarely into the armhole.

A Summer Sweater _(see illustration on front cover)_

To fit bust	ins.	34	36	38	40
	cms.	86	91	96	101
Sleeve seam	ins.	15	15	15	15
	cms.	38	38	38	38
Patons Fiona					
✕50grm.balls		9	10	11	11

No. 8 crochet hook. One buckle.

Tension: 10½ sts. to 2 ins. (5 cms.) and 8 rows to 3 ins. (8 cms.).

This garment has been specially designed for the size range given and it is regretted that no other adaptations are available.

Note: Owing to nature of pattern the turning ch. at beg. of 2nd patt. row is an extra st. and is not counted in the st. checks.
Back: Make 95 [99, 107, 111] ch.
Foundation row—1 tr. in 4th ch. from hook, 1 tr. in each ch. to end, turn (93 [97, 105, 109] sts.).
Work in **patt.** as follows:—
1st row—(**Wrong side**), 3 ch., miss 1st st., working into front loop **only** work 1 tr. in each st. to end, turn.
2nd row—4 ch., y.o.h., draw loop through 1st st., draw loop through 2 loops on hook (y.o.h., draw loop through next st., draw loop through 2 loops) 3 times (5 loops on hook), draw loop through all 5 loops, *3 ch., (y.o.h., draw loop through next st., draw loop through 2 loops) 4 times, draw loop through all loops, rep. from *to last st., 2 ch., 1 tr. in last st., turn.
3rd row—3 ch., miss 2 sts., 3 tr. in next st., *miss 3 sts., 4 tr. in next st., rep. from*, ending 1 tr. in 3rd of 4 turning ch., turn.
4th row—3 ch., miss 1st st., 1 tr. in each st. to end, turn.
These 4 rows form patt.
Continue in patt. until 10 complete patts. have been worked, then rep. the 1st patt. row again.

Shape armholes as follows:—
1st row—s.s. across 4 sts., patt. to last 5 sts., 2 ch., 1 tr. in next st., turn.
2nd row—In patt.
3rd and 4th rows—s.s. across 2 sts., patt. to last 2 sts., turn.

5th row—As 1st row (69 [73, 81, 85] sts.).
3rd and 4th sizes only
6th, 7th and 8th rows—As 2nd, 3rd and 4th rows ([73, 77] sts.).

All sizes**
Continue on these sts. until Back measures approximately 23½ [24, 24, 24½] ins. 59 [61, 61, 62] cms., ending with a 3rd [4th, 4th, 1st] patt. row. Fasten off.

Front: Work as Back to**.
Work 7 [7, 4, 4] rows, thus ending with a 1st patt. row.
Divide for neck as follows:—
Next row—Patt. across 20 sts., 2 ch., 1 tr. in next st., turn.
Work straight on these 21 sts. until Front measures same as Back.
Fasten off.
Leaving centre 27 [31, 31, 35] sts. free, rejoin yarn to next st. and complete to match first half.

SLEEVES
Make 47 [51, 55, 59] ch. and work foundation row as on Back (45 [49, 53, 57] sts.).
Work rows 1 to 3 of patt. as on Back.
Shape sides as follows:—
***Next row—3 ch., 1 tr. in first st., 1 tr. in each st. to last st., 2 tr. in last st., turn.
Next row—3 ch., working into front loop **only**, 1 tr. in first st., work 1 tr. in each st. to end, ending 2 tr. in last st., turn (49 [53, 57, 61] sts.).
Work 6 rows in patt. ***
Rep. from *** to *** once more, then work inc. rows again.
Work 2 rows straight, then work inc. rows again.
Rep. these 4 rows twice more (69 [73, 77, 81] sts.).
Work 4 rows straight, thus ending with a 1st patt. row (9 complete patts., plus 1st row).

Shape top by working rows 1 to 4 of armhole shaping as on Back 3 times (21 [25, 29, 33] sts.).
3rd and 4th sizes only
Rep. 1st row once more ([21, 25] sts.).

All sizes: Fasten off.

Continued from Page 57

A Summer Sweater

BELT
Make 155 [159, 163, 167] ch. and work foundation row as on Back (153 [157, 161, 165] sts.).
Work 1st patt. row, then work 4th patt. row, then 1st row again. Fasten off.

TO MAKE UP
With wrong side of work facing, press each piece using a **cool** iron and **dry** cloth.
Join shoulder, side and sleeve seams, insert sleeves.
With right side facing, work 1 row d.c. round neck, turn and work another row in d.c.
Fasten off.
Attach buckle to Belt.
Press seams.

(Paton's pattern)

Pinafore Dress

Materials: 12 [13, 13, 14] balls (50 gram) Patons Double Knitting.
No. 4 00 mm (8) and No. 3.50 mm (9) crochet hooks.
Measurements: To fit bust 32-33 [34-35, 36-37, 38-39] in. (81-84 [86-89, 91-94, 96-99] cm). Length from top of shoulders approx., 37 [37½, 38, 38½] in. (94 [95, 96, 98] cm) adjustable.
Tension: 9 sts. and 4 rows to 2 in. (5 cm) measured over trebles on No. 4.00 hook.
Special Note: dec. 2 = (y.o.h., draw loop through next stitch, y.o.h., draw loop through first 2 loops on hook) 3 times, y.o.h., draw loop through all 4 loops on hook (thus making 1 st. from 3).

BACK
** With No. 3.50 hook, make 107 [112, 117, 122] ch.
Foundation row—1 d.c. in 2nd ch. from hook, 1 d.c. in each ch. to end (106 [111, 116, 121] sts.).
Change to No. 4.00 hook and work as follows:—
1st row—(Right side), 3 ch., miss first st., 1 tr. in each following st. to end (3 ch. counts as first st.).
Rep. last row 4 times more (adjust length here).
Work patt. band as follows:—
1st row—1 ch., 1 d.c. in first st., * 4 ch., miss 4 sts., 1 d.c. in next st., rep. from * to end.

2nd row—5 ch., 4 tr. in first 4 ch. sp., * 2 ch., 4 tr. in next 4 ch. sp., rep. from *, ending 1 ch., 1 d.tr. in last d.c.
3rd row—1 ch., 1 d.c. in 1 ch. sp., * 4 ch., 1 d.c. in next 2 ch. sp., rep. from *, ending last rep. 4 ch., 1 d.c. in last ch. sp.
4th row—3 ch., 4 tr. in first 4 ch. sp., * 1 tr. in next d.c., 4 tr. in next 4 ch. sp., rep. from *, ending 1 tr. in last d.c.
These 4 rows form patt. band.
Work 6 rows straight in tr.
Work 4 rows of patt. band.
*** **1st dec. row**—3 ch., miss first st., 1 tr. in each of next 11 [12, 13, 14] sts., dec. 1, 1 tr. in each of next 12 [13, 14, 15] sts., dec. 1, 1 tr. in each st. to last 28 [30, 32, 34] sts., (dec. 1, 1 tr. in each of next 12 [13, 14, 15] sts.) twice.
Work 1 row in tr.

2nd dec. row—3 ch., miss first st., 1 tr. in each of next 11 [12, 13, 14] sts., dec. 1, 1 tr. in each st. to last 14 [15, 16, 17] sts., dec. 1, 1 tr. in each st. to end.
Work 1 row in tr.

3rd dec. row—As 1st dec. row.
Work 1 row in tr. (96 [101, 106, 111] sts.).
Work 4 rows of patt. band. ***

Pinafore Dress

Continued

Work from *** to *** twice more (76 [81, 86, 91] sts.).

Work 6 rows straight in tr.

Work 4 rows of patt. band.

Work straight in tr. until Back measures approx. 29 in. (73 cm), ending with right side facing.

Shape armholes as follows:—

1st row—S.s. over 4 sts., 3 ch., miss first st., 1 tr. in each following st. to last 4 sts., turn.

2nd row—3 ch., miss first st., dec. 2, 1 tr. in each st. to last 4 sts., dec. 2, 1 tr. in top of 3 ch. **
Rep. last row until 48 [53, 54, 59] sts. remain.

2nd and 4th sizes only:—

Next row—3 ch., miss first st., dec. 1, 1 tr. in each st. to last 3 sts., dec. 1, 1 tr. in top of 3 ch. ([51, 57] sts.).

All sizes:—

Work straight in tr. until Back measures approx. 37 [37½, 38, 38½] in. (94 [95, 96, 98] cm), ending with right side facing.

Shape shoulders as follows:—

Next row—S.s. over 2 [2, 3, 3] sts., 1 d.c. in each of next 2 [3, 3, 3] sts., 1 h.tr. in each of next 3 sts., 1 tr. in each of next 3 [3, 3, 4] sts.
Fasten off.

With right side facing, leave centre 28 [29, 30, 31] sts. unworked, rejoin yarn in next st. and make 3 ch., miss this st., 1 tr. in each of next 2 [2, 2, 3] sts., 1 h.tr. in each of next 3 sts., 1 d.c. in each of next 2 [3, 3, 3] sts.
Fasten off.

FRONT

Work as for Back from ** to **.

Divide for neck as follows:—

1st row—3 ch., miss first st., dec. 2, 1 tr. in each of next 14 [16, 18, 20] sts., turn (16 [18, 20, 22] sts.).

Continue on these sts. for first side as follows:—

2nd row—3 ch., miss first st., 1 tr. in each st. to last 4 sts., dec. 2, 1 tr. in top of 3 ch.

3rd row—3 ch., miss first st., dec. 2, 1 tr. in each st. to end.

4th row—As 2nd row.

Rep. 3rd row 0 [0, 1, 1] time more (10 [12, 12, 14] sts.).

2nd side only:—

Next row—3 ch., miss first st., dec. 1, 1 tr. in each st. to end (11 sts.).

4th size only:—

Next row—3 ch., miss first st., 1 tr. in each st. to last 3 sts., dec. 1, 1 tr. in top of 3 ch. (13 sts.).

All sizes:—

Work straight in tr. until Front matches Back at armhole edge, ending with right side facing.

Shape shoulder as follows:—

Next row—S.s. over 2 [2, 3, 3] sts., 1 d.c. in each of next 2 [3, 3, 3] sts., 1 h.tr. in each of next 3 sts., 1 tr. in each of last 3 [3, 3, 4] sts.
Fasten off.

With right side facing, leave centre 28 [29, 30, 31] sts. unworked, rejoin yarn in next st. and make 3 ch., miss this st., 1 tr. in each st. to last 4 sts., dec. 2, 1 tr. in top of 3 ch.

Finish to correspond with first side, reversing shapings.

TO MAKE UP

With wrong side of work facing, press each piece lightly using a warm iron and damp cloth.

Using a flat seam, join shoulder and side seams. Press seams.

With right side facing, and No. 3.50 hook, work 3 rounds d.c. all round each armhole.

With right side facing, and No. 3.50 hook, work 3 rounds d.c. all round neck, decreasing 1 st. at corners on Front on every row.

(Paton's pattern)

60

Jacket in Arran style

Like any Arran type work, this is complicated, though very interesting and rewarding once it is set up, using varied entries which must be followed, to get the desired effect in the finished garment.

Materials:

38 inch chest	34 balls
40 inch chest	36 balls
42 inch chest	38 balls in 25 grms.

Robin Rondo Double Knitting.
Hook 350(9) and Hook 450(7). 24 inch open ended Zip.

Tension: Moss stitch—9 stitches to 2 inches, 9 rows to 2 inches.
Taken from Clusters—5 clusters to 2¼ inches, 2 rows to 1 inch.

Special Note: Cluster = cl:—Work as tr, retaining last loop on the hook, make another in the same place, till 3 loops on the hook. y.r.h. draw through all 3 loops. After first row, the entry into the cluster is under the third thread (like stem entry). When the 2 foundation rows have been done, the instructions will read for the right, centre, and left panels only, the other stitches between worked in all clusters, then only right and left panels.

Back: With hook 350(9), ch 85/89/93 sts. Into 3rd st from hook 1dc, * miss 1 st, 1 ch 1dc into next st*. Repeat**.

Pattern row for Moss Stitch: 3 ch for the turn, 1 dc into ch sp. * miss st, into ch sp -1 ch 1dc. * Repeat**. When work measures 2½ inches change to hook 450(7) and Arran.

1st Foundation row: 3 ch for the turn. Under each of the next 5/5/6 ch sps- work cl. **Right Panel:** 1 tr into dc, make cross (miss ch sp, 1 tr into dc, hold this at the front, 1 tr into missed ch sp). Counting sp and st as singles, into the next 10 1 tr, cross, 1 tr, . . . end of panel. Under each of the next 5/6/6 ch sps, cl. **Centre Panel:** 1 tr into dc, miss sp and st, 1 1 tr into both next sp and st. Holding sts just worked at the front, 1 1 tr into each of the 2 missed places. (Twist to the front) 1 tr into sp and st, twist 4 to the back (the same as before, holding the worked stitches at

the back. 1 tr, . . . end of centre panel. Under each of the next 5/6/6 ch sps, cl. **Left Panel:** As right, . . . Under each of the next 5/5/6 ch sps, cl. End row by working 1 tr into top of ch.

2nd Foundation row: 1 cl into previous cl throughout, other than the decreasings. First panel (all in st-tr) 1 bk, cross, 1 bk, 1 fwd, 2 bk, 2 fwd, 2 bk, 1 fwd, 1 bk, cross, 1 bk. Central Panel. 12 bk. Second Panel as first.

Pattern

1st row: Right Panel: 1 tr fwd, cross, 1 tr fwd, 1 tr bk, 1 tr (between st just worked over and next) miss 4 sts, 1 1 tr into next 2 sts, holding the last 2 sts worked at the front, 1 1 tr fwd round first 2 missed sts. (Twist to the front) 1 tr (between sts) 1 tr bk, 1 tr fwd, cross, 1 tr fwd . . . **Centre Panel:** 1 tr fwd, miss 2 sts, 1 1 tr into next 2 sts, holding these at the front, 1 1 tr fwd into 2 missed sts. (Twist to the front). 2 tr fwd, twist 4 sts, this time holding them to the back. 1 tr fwd, . . . **Left Panel:** As right except for the twist, hold the sts at the back.

2nd row—All in tr's over panels. 1 bk, 1 cross, 1 bk, 2 fwd, 4 bk, 2 fwd, 1 bk, cross, 1 bk, Centre Panel 12 bk. (The centre panel is a repeat of rows 1 and 2 throughout. Left Panel as right.

3rd row—**Right Panel:** 1 tr fwd, cross, 1 tr fwd, 2 tr bk, twist 4 to the front, as in centre panel, 2 tr bk, 1 tr fwd cross, 1 tr fwd. Left Panel the same as right only twist to the back.

4th row—As 2nd row.

5th row—**Right Panel:** 1 tr fwd, cross, 1 tr fwd, 1 tr bk, miss 1 st, 2 tr fwd, between 2nd and 3rd st of previous row, 2 tr, 2 tr fwd, miss 1 st, 1 tr bk, 1 tr fwd, 1 cross, 1 tr fwd. Left Panel as right.

6th row—Both Panels all in tr's. 1 bk, cross, 1 bk, 1 fwd, 2 bk, 2 fwd, 2 bk, 1 fwd, 1 bk, 1 cross, 1 bk.

7th row—Both panels alike all in tr's. 1 tr fwd, 1 cross, 1 fwd, 1 bk, 2 fwd, 2 bk, 2 fwd, 1 bk, 1 fwd, 1 cross, 1 fwd.

8th row—As 6th.
Repeat these 8 rows 3 times more.

Armhole decreasings: Keeping to pattern, ss over to 4/4/5 cl, work 3 ch, work to within 3/3/4 cl, 1 tr turn.

Jacket in Arran style

Continued

2nd row—ss over 1 cl, work row to the same place the other side, ending with 1 tr.
Continue straight till 2 complete patterns have been worked. Cast off.

Right Side: With hook 350(9) ch 43/45/47 sts. Work welt in Moss Stitch as back, change to hook 450(7).
Foundation row: 3 ch for the turn. Into ch sp, 1 tr, miss st and sp, 1 1 tr into next st and sp, holding sts at the back, work 1 1 tr into missed places, 1 tr into dc. Into each of the next 5/6/6 ch sps, cl. Work as left panel, with 5/5/6 cl at the end and 1 tr.
2nd Foundation row and all rows, as main, working the left panel, and half centre, holding sts at the back when working the twist. Decrease on the left side as in main, when 4 full patterns have been worked.
Complete full pattern of 8 rows.
Neck: ss over to 2nd cl, work 3 ch and row.
Next row—Work across to 2/3/3 cluster after panel.
Next row—ss over 1 cluster. Continue on these sts to complete the pattern, cast off.

Left side: Work as right side for moss st. Change hook and work pattern as right panel and half centre panel. (Twisting to the front) ending row with 1 bk, and 1 tr into top of last st.

Collar: Sew shoulder seams together. With right side of work facing you, and hook 350(9) join yarn at neck edge and work 3 ch. Work 23/24/25 tr's to shoulder, 18/19/20 tr's across back neck, 24/25/25 down other side. Work 7 rows in single rib i.e. 1 tr fwd, 1 tr bk, change to hook 450(7) and work a further 7 rows. Cast off. Sew in all ends. Work 1 round of dc's, starting at base of collar, working twice into corners, completely round garment, which will form a binding, and once more round collar only. Cast off. Sew in end, and sew Zip on the fronts.

Sleeves: 2 alike.
With hook 350(9) ch 41 sts, for all sizes. Work welt $2\frac{1}{2}$ inches. Change to hook 450(7) and pattern. This is only worked over 2 rows, entry into moss st as back. 7 cl, centre panel, 7 cl. Increase on the 3rd and fourth rows thus.
3rd row—After ch turn 1 tr into its base, and work 2 tr's at the very end.
4th row—Make the turn, and 1 cl between 2 tr's, repeat at the other end, 1 tr into the end. Repeat these 4 rows, till 14 cl's each side of centre panel. Work straight to $18\frac{1}{2}$, $19\frac{1}{2}$, $20\frac{1}{2}$ inches.

Decrease by ss over 2 cluster, work to within 2 clusters, turn. Repeat till 2 cl's remain each side of the centre panel. Cast off.
To finish. Backstitch all seams, insert sleeves with backstitch.
Press work on the wrong side with a damp cloth. Turn to right side fold over collar, lightly press.
AVOID PRESSING WELTS.

Cover ups

(see full colour illustration facing page 48)

Lace Pattern

Materials: 5 balls (50g), PATONS BRILLIANTE DOUBLE KNITTING, 100% Bri-Nylon. No. 6 (5.00 mm) and No. 9 (3.50 mm) crochet hooks.

Measurements: Length, 20 in. (51 cm).

Tension: 1 rep. of border patt. = 5½ in. (14 cm); 4 rows = 3 in. (7 cm).

Note: Cl.s = * (y.r.h.) twice, draw loop through next d.tr., (y.r.h., draw loop through 2 loops on hook) twice; rep. from * 4 times more, y.r.h., draw loop through all 6 loops on hook, 1 ch.

Back and Front alike: With No. 6 hook, start at lower edge with 198 ch. and work border patt.:

1st row—1 d.tr. in 6th ch. from hook, 1 ch., 1 d.tr. in same ch., * (miss 1 ch., 1 ch., 1 d.tr. in next ch.) 12 times, (1 ch., 1 d.tr. in same ch.) 4 times, (thus working 5 d.tr. in same st.); rep. from * 6 times (miss 1 ch., 1 ch., 1 d.tr. in next ch.) 12 times, (1 ch., 1 d.tr. in same ch.) twice, turn with 5 ch.

2nd row—* (1 d.tr. in next d.tr., 1 ch.) 5 times, Cl.5, (1 d.tr. in next d.tr., 1 ch.) 6 times; rep. from * to end, working last d.tr. in 4th of 5 turning ch., turn with 5 ch.

3rd row—1 d.tr., 1 ch., 1 d.tr. in 1st d.tr., * (1 ch., 1 d.tr. in next d.tr.) 12 times, (1 ch., 1 d.tr. in same st.) 4 times; rep. from *6 times, (1 ch., 1 d.tr. in next d.tr.) 11 times, (1 ch., 1 d.tr. in 4th of 5 turning ch.) 3 times, turn with 5 ch.

4th row—As 2nd, omitting turning ch.

5th row—1 d.c. in 1st d.tr., *miss 1 d.tr., 3 ch., 1 d.c., 9 ch., 1 d.c. all in next d.tr. (thus making a ch. loop), miss 1 d.tr., 3 ch., 1 d.c., 11 ch., 1 d.c. all in next d.tr., miss 1 d.tr., 3 ch., 1 d.c., 13 ch., 1 d.c. all in next d.tr., miss 1 d.tr., 3 ch., 1 d.c., 11 ch., 1 d.c. all in next d.tr., miss 1 d.tr., 3 ch., 1 d.c., 9 ch., 1 d.c. all in next d.tr., miss 1 d.tr., 3 ch., 1 d.c. in next d.tr.; rep. from *to end, work last d.c. in 4th of 5 turning ch.

6th row—1 d.c. in 1st d.c., *7 ch., 1 d.c. in each of 5 ch. loops, 7 ch., 1 d.c. in next d.c.; rep. from *to end, turn with 5 ch. This completes border patt. Cont. in centre patt.:

1st row—1 d.tr., 1 ch., 1 d.tr. in 1st d.c., * 6 ch., 1 d.c. in centre of 5 d.c., 6 ch., 1 d.tr., (1 ch., 1 d.tr.) 4 times all in single d.c.; rep. from *6 times, 6 ch., 1 d.c. in centre of 5 d.c., 6 ch., 1 d.tr., (1 ch., 1 d.tr.) twice all in last d.c., turn with 10 ch.

2nd row—* (1 d.c. in next ch. sp., 6 ch.) twice, 1 d.tr. in centre of d.tr. group, 6 ch.; rep. from * to end, work last d.tr. in 4th of 5 turning ch., turn with 5 ch.

3rd row—1 d.tr., 1 ch., 1 d.tr. in 1st d.tr., *5 ch., miss next ch. sp., 1 d.c. in next ch. sp., miss next ch. sp., 5 ch., 1 d.tr., (1 ch., 1 d.tr.) 4 times all in d.tr.; rep. from *6 times, 5 ch., miss next ch. sp., 1 d.c. in next ch. sp., miss next ch. sp., 5 ch., 1 d.tr., (1 ch., 1d.tr.) twice in 4th of 10 turning ch., turn with 10 ch.

Rep. 2nd and 3rd rows 3 times. Turn with 9 ch.

Shape thus:—**Next row**—*(1 d.c. in next ch. sp., 5 ch.) twice, 5 ch., 1 d.tr. in centre of d.tr. group; rep. from *to end, work last d.tr. in 4th of 5 turning ch., turn with 5 ch.

Next row—1 d.tr., 1 ch., 1 d.tr. in 1st d.tr., * 4 ch., miss next ch. sp., 1 d.c. in next ch. sp., miss next ch. sp., 5 ch., 1 d.tr., (1 ch., 1 d.tr.) 4 times all in d.tr.; rep. from *6 times, 4 ch., miss next ch. sp., 1 d.c. in next ch. sp., miss next ch. sp., 4 ch., 1 d.tr., (1 ch., 1 d.tr.) twice in 4th of 9 turning ch., turn with 9 ch.

Rep. last 2 rows once. Turn with 8 ch.

Next row—* (1 d.c. in next ch. sp., 4 ch.) twice 1 d.tr. in centre of d.tr. group, 4 ch.; rep. from * to end, work last d.tr. in 4th of 5 turning ch., turn with 5 ch.

Next row—1 d.tr., 1 ch., 1 d.tr. in 1st d.tr., * 3 ch., miss next ch. sp., 1 d.c. in next ch. sp., miss next ch. sp., 3 ch., 1 d.tr., (1 ch., 1 d.tr.) 4 times all in d.tr.; rep. from *6 times, 3 ch., miss next ch. sp., 1 d.c. in next ch. sp., miss next ch. sp., 3 ch., 1 d.tr., (1 ch., 1 d.tr.) twice in 4th of 8 turning ch., turn with 7 ch.

Next row—* (1 d.c. in next ch. sp., 3 ch.) twice, 1 d.tr. in centre of d.tr. group, of 3 ch.; rep. from *to end, but working last d.tr. in 4th of 5 turning ch., turn with 5 ch.

Pelerine *Front view* 16 points.   Pelerine *Rear view* with sun ray effect.

Waist coat and round shoulder bag in long cross.

Stole in King Solomons Knot.

Cover ups

Continued

Next row—1 d.tr., 1 ch., 1 d.tr. in 1st d.tr., * 2 ch., miss next ch. sp., 1 d.c. in next ch. sp., miss next ch. sp., 2 ch., 1 d.tr., (1 ch., 1 d.tr.) 4 times all in d.tr.; rep. from *6 times, 2 ch., miss next ch. sp., 1 d.c. in next ch. sp., miss next ch. sp., 2 ch., 1 d.tr., (1 ch., 1 d.tr.) twice in 4th of 7 turning ch.

Complete thus:—**1st row**—1 d.c. in 1st d.tr., * miss 1 d.tr., 3 ch., 1 tr. in next d.tr., 1 ch., 1 d.tr. in d.c., 1 ch., 1 tr. in next d.tr., miss 1 d.tr., 3 ch., 1 d.c. in next d.tr.; rep. from * to end, work last d.c. in 4th of 5 turning ch., turn with 5 ch.
2nd row—1 d.tr. in 3rd ch. from hook, 1 ch., 1 d.tr. in tr., 1 ch., 1 d.tr. in d.tr., 1 ch., 1 d.tr. in tr., miss 1 ch., 1 ch., 1 d.tr. in next ch., 1 ch., 1 d.tr. in d.c. Cont. thus working 1 ch., 1 d.tr. in every alt. st. of previous row, work last d.tr. in last d.c., turn with 5 ch.
3rd row—1 d.tr. in 2nd d.tr., *1 d.tr. in next d.tr., 1 ch., 1 d.tr. in next d.tr.; rep. from *to last d.tr., 1 d.tr. in 4th of 5 turning ch., turn with 4 ch.
4th row—1 d.tr. in 2nd d.tr., * 1 ch., 1 d.tr. in next d.tr., 1 d.tr. in next d.tr.; rep. from * to last d.tr., 1 ch., 1 d.tr. in 4th of 5 turning ch., turn with 4 ch.
5th row—1 d.tr. in 2nd d.tr., 1 d.tr. in each foll. d.tr., 1 d.tr. in top of turning ch.
Change to No. 9 hook. **Next row**—1 d.c. in 1st st., * miss 1 st., 1 d.c. in next st.; rep. from * to end (leave turning ch. unworked). Work 2 rows d.c. Fasten off.

Using a **cool** iron and **dry** cloth, press parts lightly. Join seams. Press seams.

Grandmas' traditional crochet

Materials: 9 balls (50g) Dark, 7 balls (50g) Medium, 4 balls (50g) Light PATONS DOUBLET. No. 3 (1.25 mm) crochet hook.
Measurement: Length at side seam approx. 18 in. (46 cm). Length approx. 25 in. (63 cm).
Tension: Each Motif = 4 in. square.

MOTIF (Make 64)
Always turn work after each round.
With L., work 5 ch.; join into ring with sl.st.

1st round—With L., 3 ch., 2 tr. into ring (1 ch., 3 tr. into ring) 3 times, 1 ch., join to 3rd of 3 ch. with sl.st. Break off L.
2nd round—With M., join yarn in last 1 ch. sp. of previous round, 3 ch., 2 tr. in same sp., (1 ch., 3 tr., 2 tr. in next sp.) 3 times, 1 ch., 3 tr. in next sp. 2 ch., join to 3rd of 3 ch. with sl.st. Break off M.
3rd round—With D., join yarn in last 2 ch. sp. of previous round, 3 ch., 2 tr. in same sp., (1 ch., 3 tr. in next sp., 1 ch., 3 tr., 2 ch., 3 tr. in next sp.) 3 times, 1 ch., 3 tr. in next sp., 1 ch., 3 tr. in next sp., 2 ch., join to 3rd of 3 ch. with sl.st. Break off D.

Using D. join 48 motifs into strip 4 × 12, and rem. 16 into square 4 × 4. Join one edge of square to top edge of 1st. 4 motifs along strip, then opposite edge of square to top edge of last 4 motifs of strip.

Neck Edging: With M. and right side facing, start at side seam and work 1 d.c. in each tr. join row to within 2 sts. of centre.
Work 1 d.c. in each of next 2 sts., leaving loops on hook, then put the yarn over the hook and pull through all loops on hook (1 st. decrease—from now on referred to as dec.1), dec.1, work 1 d.c. in each tr., and joining row to within 2 sts. of centre (dec.1) twice, work 1 d.c. in each tr., and joining row to end of round, join to 1st d.c. with sl.st.

Next round—Work 1 ch., 1 d.c. in each st. to within 2 sts. of centre, (dec.1) twice, 1 d.c. in each st. to within 2 sts. of centre, (dec.1) twice, 1 d.c. in each st. to end of round, join to top of ch. st. with a sl.st. Rep. last round twice. Fasten off.

Lower Edging: With M. and right side facing, start at side seam and work 1 d.c. in each tr. joining row and sp. to within 1 st. of centre (work 2 d.c. in next st.) twice, work 1 d.c. in each tr. joining row and sp. to within 1 st. of centre (work 2 d.c. in next st.) twice, work 1 d.c. into each tr. joining row and sp. to end of round, join to 1st d.c. with sl.st.

Next round—Work 1 ch., 1 d.c. in each st. to within 1 st. of centre (work 2 d.c. in next st.) twice, 1 d.c. in each st. to within 1 st. of centre, (work 2 d.c. in next st.) twice, work 1 d.c. in each st. to end of round, join to top of ch.st. with sl.st. Rep. last round twice. Fasten off. Press lightly.

Disco Dress

(see full colour illustration facing page 32)

To fit bust			
	in.	30	32
	cm.	76	81

Length from back of neck to point of skirt excluding fringes			
	in.	36½	37½
	cm.	93	95

Patons Brilliante Double Knitting,
100% Bri-Nylon × 50 gram balls 8 9

No. 8 (4.00 mm) crochet hook. 5 buttons.

Tension:
9 sts. = 2 in. (5 cm) in width.
8 rows = 3 in. (7 cm) in depth.

This garment has been specially designed for the size range given and it is regretted that no adaptations are available.

BACK
Skirt
Make 5 ch.

1st row—3 tr. into 4th ch. from hook, 3 tr. into last ch., turn with 3 ch.

2nd row—1 tr. into each of first 2 tr., 3 tr. into each of next 2 tr., 1 tr. into each of last 2 tr., turn with 3 ch.

3rd row—1 tr. into each of first 4 tr., 3 tr. into each of next 2 tr., 1 tr. into each of last 4 tr., turn with 3 ch.

4th row—1 tr. into each of first 6 tr., 3 tr. into each of next 2 tr., 1 tr. into each of last 6 tr., turn with 3 ch.

5th row—1 tr. into each of first 8 tr., 3 tr. into each of next 2 tr., 1 tr. into each of last 8 tr., turn with 3 ch.

6th row—1 tr. into first tr., *1 ch., miss 1 tr., 1 tr. into next tr.*, rep. from * to * 3 times more, 1 ch., miss 1 tr., 3 tr. into each of next 2 tr., now rep. from * to * to end, turn with 3 ch.

Continue in this way, inc. in centre of every row, and making openwork insertion on every 6th row until there are 154 [158] sts., omitting turning ch. at end of last row for **1st size only.** (The 2nd [3rd] row of the 7th patt. from start should now be completed).

2nd size
Next row—Work 76 sts., (tr. 3 tog.) twice, work to end, turn.

Both sizes
Next row—s.s. over first 5 sts., 2 ch., work 69 sts., tr.3 tog., turn with 2 ch.

Finish each side separately as follows:—

1st row—Tr.3 tog., work to last 4 sts., turn.

2nd row—s.s. over first 4 sts., 2 ch., work to last 3 sts., tr.3 tog., turn with 2 ch.

Rep. 1st and 2nd rows 4 times more, then 1st row once (4 sts.). Fasten off.

Rejoin yarn between the two 3 tr. groups at centre with s.s., 2 ch., tr.3 tog., work to last 5 sts., turn.

Complete to match first side.

Bodice
With right side of work facing, join yarn to waist edge at side and work 61 [65] d.c. along waist edge as follows:—

Work 30 [32] d.c. along first side to centre, working alternately 2 d.c. into one row and 3 d.c. into the next, 1 d.c. between the 2 sts. at centre, and 30 [32] d.c. along other side, turn with 2 ch.

Continue in patt. as follows:—

1st row—1 tr. into each st. to end, turn with 2 ch. This row forms the patt.

Work 4 more rows.

Inc. 1 st. at each end of next and every alt. row until there are 75 [79] sts.

Work straight until Bodice measures 8 [8½] in. (20 [21] cm) from start, ending with right side facing, and omitting turning ch. at end of last row.

Shape armholes
1st row—s.s. over first 4 [5] sts., 2 ch., tr.2 tog., work to last 6 [7] sts., tr.2 tog., turn with 2 ch. Now tr.2 tog. at each end of next 5 rows (55 [57] sts.).

Work 14 rows straight, omitting turning ch. at end of last row.

Shape shoulders and back of neck
Next row—s.s. over first 5 [6] sts., 2 ch., 1 tr. into each of next 10 sts., tr.2 tog., turn with 2 ch.

Next row—tr.2 tog., 1 tr. into each of next 4 sts. Fasten off.

Miss centre 20 sts. for neck, and rejoin yarn into the 21st st. with a s.s., 2 ch., tr.2 tog., 1 tr. into each of next 10 sts., turn.

Next row—s.s. over first 5 sts., 2 ch., 1 tr. into each of next 4 sts., tr.2 tog. Fasten off.

Front: Work Skirt as for Back.

Bodice

Left Front: With right side of work facing, join yarn to waist edge at side and work 30 [32] d.c. along first side to centre as for Back, turn with 2 ch.

Continue in patt. as follows:—

Work 5 rows.

Inc. 1 st. at side edge on next and every alt. row until there are 37 [39] sts.

Work straight until Bodice measures 8 [8½] in. (20 [21] cm) from start, ending with right side facing, and omitting turning ch. at end of last row.

Shape armhole

1st row—s.s. over first 4 [5] sts., 2 ch., tr.2 tog., work to end, turn with 2 ch.

Now tr.2 tog. at armhole edge on next 5 rows.

Work 3 rows straight, omitting turning ch. at end of last row.

Shape neck

Next row—s.s. over first 7 sts., 2 ch., tr.2 tog., work to end, turn with 2 ch.

Now tr.2 tog. at neck edge on next 4 rows.

Work 6 rows straight, omitting turning ch. at end of last row.

Shape shoulder

Next row—s.s. over first 5 [6] sts., 2 ch., 1 tr. into each st. to end, turn with 2 ch.

Next row—1 tr. into each of first 5 sts. Fasten off.

Right Front: Rejoin yarn at centre of skirt and work 30 [32] d.c. along other side, turn with 2 ch.

Continue in patt. as follows:—

Work 5 rows.

Inc. 1 st. at side edge on next and every alt. row until there are 37 [39] sts.

Work straight until Bodice measures 8 [8½] in. (20 [21] cm) from start, ending with right side facing.

Shape armhole

1st row—Work to last 6 [7] sts., tr.2 tog., turn with 2 ch.

Now tr.2 tog. at armhole edge on next 5 rows.

Work 3 rows straight.

Shape neck

Next row—Work to last 9 sts., tr.2 tog., turn with 2 ch.

Now tr.2 tog. at neck edge on next 4 rows.

Work 6 rows straight.

Shape shoulder

Next row—Work to last 5 [6] sts., turn.

Next row—s.s. over first 5 sts., 2 ch., 1 tr. into each of last 5 sts. Fasten off.

TO MAKE UP AND BORDERS

Press lightly with a warm iron and damp cloth. Join shoulder and side seams.

Front opening and neck border

Join yarn to Right Front opening edge at waist with a d.c., and work a row of d.c. up this edge, round neck and down Left Front opening edge, working 2 d.c. for each row, and 1 d.c. for each st., turn with 1 ch.

Now work another row of d.c. all round, inc. at corners of neck as required to keep work flat, making 5 buttonloops along Right Front opening edge by working 2 ch. and missing 1 st.; the top loop should come at start of neck shaping, the bottom loop 2 in. (5 cm) from waist, and the rest equally spaced between.

Fasten off.

Overlap edges and sew neatly at waist.

Armhole borders

Join yarn to underarm at side seam, and work 2 rows d.c. round armholes in same way, turning with 1 ch. at end of first row. Fasten off.

Lower border

Join yarn to lower edge of skirt at right side seam with a d.c., and work a row of d.c. along front and back, working 2 d.c. for each row.

Next round—1 d.c. into first d.c., *5 ch., miss 3 d.c., 1 d.c. into next d.c., rep. from * to end.

Next round—s.s. over first 2 ch., 1 d.c. into next ch., *5 ch., 1 d.c. into centre ch. of 5 ch. loop, rep. from*, ending 1 d.c. into first d.c. Rep last round once more. Fasten off.

Fringe

Using 6 strands of yarn 11 in. (28 cm) long for each tassel, work a fringe along Lower Border edge, working a tassel into each ch. loop. Press seams. Sew on buttons. Trim fringes.

(Paton's pattern)

Unusual Cushion

Like the Pelerine, differing in the centre and on the increases.

Material: 3 ounces of Yellow, 3 ounces of Pink, 2 of Purple. Hayfield Croft. Hook 350(9).
Starting at the centre in Yellow.
Ch 4 sts. ss to the 1st to form a ring.

1st round—Into this ring, 3 ch 1 tr, * 1 ch 2 tr * Repeat **. 4 times more, 1 ch, ss to 3rd ch.

2nd round—Turn work completely on this round and every round. ss under ch sp to the starting point on each round. 3 ch 1 tr into first sp. * 1 tr in stm of 2 sts, under ch sp 2 tr 1 ch 2 tr. * Repeat **. 4 times more, 1 tr into stm of 2 sts, 2 tr under ch sp (completes first point) ss to 3rd ch.

3rd round—Change to purple. 3 ch 1 tr, * 1 tr into stm of 2 sts, dec over 2 sts, (once the dec has been worked it is ignored and the dec on the following round is the st each side) 2 tr into stm of 2 sts, 2 tr 1 ch 2 tr under ch sp. * Repeat all round, ending as 2nd round.

4th round—Work as 3rd, working extra st between points as tr.

5th round—Change to pink. Work as 4th, only increasing at point making 3 tr 1 ch 3 tr.
Continue as round 4 and 5 till side is completed.
Changing colour after 6 pink, 2 purple and 2 yellow.
Other side is the same, reversing the yellow and pink colours. Join together with dc, leave opening for inner cushion and complete in dc when stuffed. When making the inner cushion pack the points evenly.

A Coat in Shell

There are other ways of obtaining the right size, without using extra stitches, and this coat is one example. Here, different size hooks are used, so you must make a sample piece first, to ensure the garment will have the correct fit when completed.

Material: 12 balls (50gr) Patons Promise for all sizes.

Hooks for 33 inch bust   400(8) 350(9) 250(12)
           35 inch bust   450(7) 400(8) 300(10)
           37 inch bust   500(6) 450(7) 350(9)
2 buttons 1 inch across.

Tension: To make a sample use 40 chs.

Width	hook 400(8)	3 patterns to 5 inches
	450(7)	3 patterns to 5½ inches
	500(6)	3 patterns to 6 inches
Length	400(8)	4 rows to 1¾ inches
	450(7)	4 rows to 2 inches
	500(6)	4 rows to 2¼ inches

Special Note: Back and fronts are made in one piece to the armholes and the work is then divided, 5 scallops for side, 10 for back, 5 for the other side. A Pattern is a shell and a twist, a scallop is half a twist 1 shell half a twist.

Back and Fronts: With 400/450/500 hook ch 145 sts, loosely and evenly.

Foundation row: Which is rather trying.
Into 5th st from hook 1 l tr, hold this to the back, 1 l tr into 4th st from hook (twist off 2 sts) * miss 2 sts, 5 tr's into next, miss 3 sts, 1 l tr into next, hold this at the back, 1 l tr into 3rd missed st, (twist). * Repeat ** ending row by working l tr into last st.

1st pattern row: 3 ch for the turn and first st, on this row and every row. * l tr bk into each of the next 2 sts, 5 tr's into the st of 3 st of sh * Repeat ** ending row with 2 tr's bk and l tr into top of ch.

2nd pattern row: After turn, * miss 1 st, 1 l tr fwd into next, which is held at the back, 1 l tr fwd into missed st. (Twist) 5 tr's into 3rd (stm entry) of sh * Repeat ** ending row with a twist and l tr into top of ch.
Continue in these 2 rows till work measures 15 inches, change to 350/400/450 hook to 20 inches, ending with 1st pattern row.

Armhole division: Work across 4 scallops, and 3 tr only into next sh, turn. Next row after the turn ch has been made, work straight into the twist. Continue on these 4 scallops till work measures 5½/6/6½ inches, shape neck. If ending at the front, ss over 1st scallop, omitting ch turn, work over 3. Turn work over 2 scallops, turn and work back 1 cast off.
If ending at the armhole edge, work across 3 scallops, turn ss over 1 scallop work 2. Turn ss over 1 scallop work 1 cast off.

Back: Join yarn into middle of shell, work 3 tr's, 8 scallops, and 3 tr's into last shell. Make the turn ch and straight into twist, work row, ending by working l tr only into half shell. Continue in pattern on these 8 scallops for 7/7½/8 inches. ss over 1 scallop, work to within 1 scallop, cast off.
Other side: Work as first side, reversing all shapings.
Sleeves: Making 2 alike.
With 500/450/400 hook ch 60 sts loosely and evenly.
Foundation row: Into 4th ch from the hook 2 tr, (making half a shell) as other foundation row making 7 scallops, and 3 tr's into last st.
Work in pattern rows, with the half a shell at each end for 17/17½/18 inches.

Armholes decreases: Over 2 rows.
1st row—ss to centre of first twist work 7 scallops and end by working ldc into twist, turn.
2nd row—ss over to centre of shell, make half shell, work across row, ending with half shell.
Repeat these 2 rows twice more, cast off.

Collar: Backstitch the shoulder seams. With right side of work facing you, and hook 250/300/350, join on yarn, working in 2nd pattern row, 3 scallops to the shoulder, 4 across the back, 3 down other side.
Work 6 rows starting at 2nd pattern row again. The pattern will then fall on the right side with the fold back of the collar.
Change to 400/450/500 hook and work another 6 rows, cast off. Sew in all ends.

Continued from Page 71

A Coat in Shell

To complete: Turn work round to the bottom, join yarn at the 6th twist along, work 1 ch. Into the centre st of scallop, work 7 l tr, work ldc into twist. Repeat this shell all round, working 1 dc at the corners, and using the twist as a guide for the shells on the sides. Oversew the side seams of sleeves, insert into the main with backstitch. Crochet the shell round the bottom of the sleeves.

To cover the buttons: Using the smallest hook, ch 3, ss to join into this work 15 tr's. Cast off. Make a second, DO NOT CAST OFF, lay on top of the first and join round with 10 dc's, insert button or disc complete with 5 more dc's. Cast off. Sew in end. Make another to match, and stitch to coat. After making a ch of 3 inches, work all round it in dc join the two ends, and twist into a figure of eight. Sew onto one button.

Very lightly press on the wrong side under a **dry** cloth and **cool** iron.

Shirt

Materials:

size 36 inch chest	15 balls	
38 inch chest	16 balls	in 24.3 grm.
40 inch chest	17 balls	Robin Tricel and Nylon PERLE

Hook 300(10)   2 small buttons.

Tension: 9 stitches to 2 inches; 5 rows to 2 inches.

Back: Ch 83/87/91 sts. Special note. The garment is made entirely in the stitch treble, after the rib has been worked. All entry of the main is in STEM. 3 ch is the turn and also replaces first st.

Foundation row: 1 s.tr into each st, starting at the third from the hook.

Work 6 rows in single rib, using s.tr working round the upright bar of the stitch.

Change to tr, after first row, stem entry 82/86/90 working sts. Pattern for 16 inches.

Armhole decreases:

1st row—ss over 6, 7, 8 sts, work to within 6, 7, 8 sts, turn.

2nd row—After ch turn, dec 2 sts, work to the last 3 sts, dec 2 sts, work last.

Repeat 2nd row twice more.

Continue straight till work measures 7, 7½, 8 inches from dec.

Shape shoulder. ss over 7 sts, work to within 7 sts turn. Repeat once, cast off.

Front: As back till work measures 14 inches.

Laceholes and Division: Work 38/40/42 sts, miss 1 st 1 ch, l tr into next 2sts, turn. Work 3 rows across these sts, making l tr into the ch.

Make the lacehole on every 4th row front edge, at the same time after 16 inches from bottom, work armhole decrease the other side. After 5½, 6, 6½ inches from armhole decrease, shape neck at front. Work to the last 9 sts, turn.

Shirt

Continued

Next row—After ch turn dec 2 sts, complete row. Repeat the dec of 2 sts at the neck side once more. Work to the same length as the back, ss over 7 sts, complete row.

Next row—Work to the last 7 sts. Cast off. Make the other side to match, reversing all shapings.

Sleeves: Making 2 alike.

Ch 57/61/65 sts.

Work rib as back and foundation tr row.

Next row, and every other row: Work twice into first and last st. Continue in this way, till work measures 7 inches. Decrease as the armholes. Cast off.

Collar: Backstitch the shoulder seams on the wrong side. With right side of work facing you join in yarn at front neck edge. Work 18/20/22 sts to the shoulder seam, 1 st into each along the back, 18/20/22 sts down to the other side. Work 8 rows in tr's, working twice into first and last stitch on every other row. Work round collar and each side of lace holes in dc's, ss to join cast off. Sew in all ends. Oversew the side seams, and sleeve seams, insert sleeve in to main garment in backstitch.

Lace: Make 3 ch, into first st of ch, work cluster of 4. i.e. work as in tr, retaining the last loop of each on the hook. y.r.h. draw through all loops.

1st link—3 ch 1 tr into top of cluster. 2nd and every link for 45 inches, 3 ch, 1 tr between the ch and st of previous link. Make another cluster at the other end. Cast off. Sew in end. Thread through the laceholes. Sew on the 2 buttons, using the space between the st for the buttonhole.

A Casual Jacket

(See full colour illustration page 33)

To fit bust	ins.	33–35	36–38
Length from top of shoulders	ins.	22	23
Sleeve seam (adjustable)	ins.	16½	17
Patons Limelight Double Crepe			
✕50 grams	balls	9	10
Patons Totem Double Crepe			
✕50 grams	balls	10	11

Note: Alt = Alternate.

A No. 10 and No. 9 crochet hook. 5 button moulds and 1 press stud.

Tension: 2 patterns = 3½ ins. in width, 4 rows = 2 ins. in height on No. 9 hook.

This garment has been specially designed for the size range given and it is regretted that no other adaptations are available.

Back: With No. 9 hook, make 83 [91] ch.

1st row—(Wrong side), 1 tr. in 4th ch. from hook, 1 tr. in each remaining ch., turn (81 [89] sts.).

2nd row—3 ch., miss 1st tr., 1 tr. in each remaining tr., ending 1 tr. in top of 3 ch., turn.

3rd and 4th rows—As 2nd row.

5th row—4 ch., 1 tr. in 1st tr., * 1 ch., miss 3 tr., (2 tr. 1 ch. 2 tr.) in next tr., 1 ch., miss 3 tr., (1 tr. 1 ch. 1 tr.) in next tr., rep. from * ending last rep. in top of 3 ch., turn.

6th row—4 ch., 1 tr. in sp. between first 2 tr., * 1 ch., (2 tr. 1 ch. 2 tr.) in sp. at centre of 4 tr., 1 ch., (1 tr. 1 ch. 1 tr.) in sp. at centre of 2 tr., rep. from *ending last rep. 1 tr. in last sp., 1 ch., 1 tr. in 3rd of 4 ch., turn (103 [113] sts.).

The 6th rows forms patt.

Continue in patt. until Back measures 14 ins., ending with right side facing.

SHAPE ARMHOLES

Next row—s.s. over 3 sts., patt. to last 3 sts., turn. Work 5 [6] rows more in patt. dec. 2 sts. at each end of every row (77 [83] sts.).

Continue straight in patt. until Back measures 21½ [22½] ins., ending with right side facing.

SHAPE SHOULDERS

1st and 2nd rows—s.s. across 9 [10] sts., patt. to last 9 [10] sts., turn.

Fasten off.

A casual Jacket

Continued

Right Front: With No. 9 hook, make 40 [43] ch. Work 1st to 4th rows as on Back (38 [41] sts.).**

1st size only
5th row—4 ch., 1 tr. in 1st tr., *1 ch., miss 3 tr., (2 tr. 1 ch. 2 tr.) in next tr., 1 ch., miss 3 tr., (1 tr. 1 ch. 1 tr.) in next tr., rep. from *3 times more, 1 ch., miss 3 tr., (2 tr. 1 ch. 2 tr.) in next tr., 1 tr. in top of 3 ch., turn.
6th row—3 ch., (2 tr. 1 ch. 2 tr.) in sp. at centre of 4 tr., *1 ch., (1 tr. 1 ch. 1 tr.) in sp. at centre of 2 tr., 1 ch., (2 tr. 1 ch. 2 tr.) in sp. at centre of 4 tr., rep. from *3 times more, 1 ch., 1 tr. in last sp., 1 ch., 1 tr. in 3rd of 4 ch., turn (50 sts.).
7th row—4 ch., 1 tr. in sp. at centre of 1st 2 tr., *1 ch., (2 tr. 1 ch. 2 tr.) in sp. at centre of 4 tr., 1 ch., (1 tr. 1 ch. 1 tr.) in sp. at centre of 2 tr., rep. from *3 times more, 1 ch., (2 tr. 1 ch. 2 tr.) in sp. at centre of 4 tr., 1 tr. in top of 3 ch., turn.
6th and 7th rows form patt.
Continue in patt. until Front measures same as Back to armhole shaping.

2nd size only
5th and 6th rows—As 5th and 6th rows on Back (53 sts.).
Rep. 6th row until Front measures same as Back to armhole shaping.

Both sizes
Shape armholes
Next row—Patt. to last 3 sts., turn. Work 5 [6] rows more in patt. dec. 2 sts. at armhole edge on every row (37 [38] sts.).
Work straight in patt. until 5 rows less than Back to shoulder shaping have been worked.

Shape neck
Next row—Patt. to last 4 [3] sts., turn.
Work 2 rows more in patt. dec. 2 sts. at neck edge on each row, then 1 st. on following 2 rows (27 [29] sts.).

Shape shoulder
1st row—Patt. to last 9 [10] sts., turn.
2nd row—s.s. over 9 [10] sts., patt. to end. Fasten off.

Left Front: Work as Right Front to**.

1st size only
5th row—3 ch., miss 1st tr., (2 tr. 1 ch. 2 tr.) in next tr., *1 ch., miss 3 tr., (1 tr. 1 ch. 1 tr.) in next tr., 1 ch., miss 3 tr., (2 tr. 1 ch. 2 tr.) in next tr., rep. from*3 times more, 1 ch., miss 3 tr., (1 tr. 1 ch. 1 tr.) in top of 3 ch., turn.
6th row—As 7th row of Right Front.
7th row—As 6th row of Right Front.
Rep. last 2 rows until Front matches Back to armhole shaping.

2nd size only
Work as Right Front to armhole shaping.

Both sizes
Shape armhole
1st row—s.s. over 3 sts., patt. to end.
Complete to match Right Front reversing all shapings.

SLEEVES
With No. 9 hook, make 37 [36] ch. loosely.

1st size only
1st row—1 tr. in 5th ch. from hook,*1 ch., miss 3 ch., (2 tr. 1 ch. 2 tr.) in next ch., 1 ch., miss 3 ch., (1 tr. 1 ch. 1 tr.) in next ch., rep. from * 3 times more, turn.
2nd and 3rd rows—As 6th row of Back (43 sts.).

2nd size only
1st row—(1 tr. 1 ch. 2 tr.) in 4th ch. from hook, *1 ch., miss 3 ch., (1 tr. 1 ch. 1 tr.) in next ch., 1 ch., miss 3 ch., (2 tr. 1 ch. 2 tr.) in next ch., rep. from*3 times more, turn.
2nd row—3 ch., (1 tr. 1 ch. 2 tr.) in sp. at centre of 4 tr.,*1 ch., (1 tr. 1 ch. 1 tr.) in sp. at centre of 2 tr., 1 ch., (2 tr. 1 ch. 2 tr.) in sp. at centre of 4 tr., rep. from*3 times more, working last tr. in top of 3 ch., turn (45 sts.).
The 2nd row forms patt.

Both sizes
Keeping patt. correct, inc. 1 st. at each end of next and every alt. row until 14 [15] inc. rows in all have been worked (71 [75] sts.).
Work 1 row straight.

A casual Jacket

Continued

Shape top
1st and 2nd rows—s.s. over 3 sts., patt. to last 3 sts., turn.
Work 9 [10] rows more in patt. dec. 2 sts. at each end of every row.
Fasten off.

CUFFS
With right side facing and No. 9 hook, work 34 [36] tr. evenly along lower edge of Sleeve, turn.
Next row—3 ch., miss 1st st., 1 tr. in each remaining st., turn.
Rep. last row until sleeve seam measures 16½ [17] ins. (adjust length here).
Fasten off.

COLLAR
With No. 9 hook, make 77 ch.
1st row—1 tr. in 5th ch. from hook,*1 ch., miss 3 ch., (2 tr. 1 ch. 2 tr.) in next ch., 1 ch., miss 3 ch., (1 tr. 1 ch. 1 tr.) in next ch., rep. from * to end, turn (93 sts.).
Work 6 rows of patt. as on Back, then work edging as follows:—
Next row—Work 1 row d.c. evenly down short side of Collar along ch. edge and up other short side of Collar, turn.
Next row—3 ch., miss 1st d.c., 1 tr. in each remaining d.c., working 3 or 4 tr. in each corner d.c. Fasten off.

LEFT FRONT BAND
With right side facing and No. 9 hook, work 1 row d.c. along front edge, turn.
Next row—3 ch., miss 1st st., 1 tr. in each st. to end, turn.
Rep. last row twice more. Fasten off.

RIGHT FRONT BAND
Work to match Left Front Band with the addition of 5 buttonholes on 2nd row of tr., the first to come ¾ inch up from lower edge, the last one ½ inch down from neck edge and remaining 3 spaced evenly between. First mark position for buttons with pins on Left Front Band to ensure even spacing, then work buttonholes to correspond as follows:—
4 ch., miss 4 sts.

BUTTON COVERS (5)
With No. 10 hook, make 2 ch., then work 6 d.c. in 2nd ch. from hook, join with s.s. to form ring.
1st round—2 d.c. in each d.c. to end of round, join with s.s.
2nd round—(1 d.c. in 1st d.c., 2 d.c. in next d.c.) 6 times, join with s.s.
3rd round—1 d.c. in each d.c. to end of round, join with s.s.
Fasten off.
Run a gathering thread around outer edge.
Cover button mould and secure ends.

TO MAKE UP
With wrong side of work facing, press each piece using a **cool** iron and **dry** cloth for yarn, a warm iron and damp cloth for wool.
Join shoulder, side and sleeve seams and stitch Sleeves in position.
Stitch Collar in position from centre of Right Front Band to centre of Left Front Band.
Press seams.
Sew on buttons.
Sew press stud at neck.

(Paton's pattern)

Tunisian Crochet

This is neither crochet or knitting, but a bit of each, a casting on and casting off loops. The hook used is different—long, with no middle thumb-piece, the same diameter all through to a knob at the end.

Patterns are limited; the fabric is a very close texture, using a larger amount of yarn.

Fig. 32 *Tunisian crochet*

1st entry known as Afghan Stitch.
Make a length of ch.
Foundation. Into each st draw yarn through, retaining all loops on the hook.
1st row, or casting off.
l ch, y.r.h. draw through 1 loop. * y.r.h. draw through 2 lps *.
2nd row. Casting on.
Into the second front thread of previous st, from right to left, draw yarn through. Repeat.

3rd row as 1st row. Casting off.
This can also be worked by crossing the stitches. Miss first st, work second, come back and work missed sts.

Fig. 33 *Second entry*

This type of stitch was seen in a suit imported from Greece, which was made of soft mohair yarn and was very expensive. To make the stitch is the same, only going through the right side of thread, to the back, yarn draw here. Looking like stocking stitch of Knitting from the front, with a very thick purl at the back.

Evolution

In the first chapter we found out how the very first yarns were spun by primitive people.

Exactly what they did with their yarns and what medium was used to make pouches and bags for domestic use was 'Hitching'. To quote the old sailors, a knot without a tie.

Most of their work was a hitch round a single thread. When this is worked round two threads, you get a finished fabric, resembling the stocking stitch of knitting, made with the aid of a sewing needle, giving it the name of Single Needle Knitting.

The back has the appearance of purl, and it is very hard to detect the difference. The front stitches are more raised from the side threads and each has a straightness, which is more curved in knitting.

A knitted stitch is drawn out through the centre of the previous one, the fabric falling below, whereas in hitching the stitch is round the outside of the previous one, the fabric coming above.

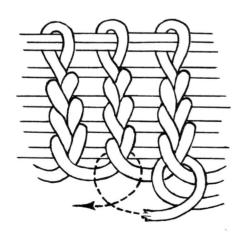

Fig. 34 *Drawing of hitching*

With the connection of the two crafts crocheting and knitting the beginnings of each had to be found.

Perhaps the word 'Knit' in the Bible really means any form of putting together of yarns, to form a fabric.

One passage mentions unravelling. Crochet and Knitting will unravel very quickly. This is not so with hitching, which leads to the belief that hitching came after crochet.

The word "Knitting" is derived from the Old English cyttan, meaning "to Knot".

Much has been lost in the history of these crafts, because the materials would have disintegrated through the passage of time.

A pair of Sandel Socks of the 4th Century in the Victoria and Albert Museum, London, were thought to be knitted. This is not so; they were made in the medium of 'Hitching'.

Where did knitting as we know it today begin? Was the use of two needles in today's craft developed towards the end of the Middle Ages around the 13th Century, when the hooks were removed and the ends pointed and knitting guilds set up. If you knit with two hooks, you will see how they catch and why the pointed ends are needed.

In the National Museum, Dublin, are to be seen wool crochet hooks of the 11th Century found in an excavation in Dublin's High Street, and very little different from those in use today.

In the craft of crochet, with its 19th Century name, we believe the oldest stitch is King Solomon's Knot of 937 BC.

In the first edition of The Sacred Craft of Knitting a passage translated from very old Hebrew manuscripts of the time of Jesus tells of a journey about to be taken by a man, with his pouch of crochet hooks on his saddle.

Give the name 'Knit' a broader meaning of 'drawing together', using a weft only to form a close texture fabric, and a great deal more can be understood.

The sacred Robe of Jesus, described as 'made from the neck down without a seam' was possibly a word picture describing the style of the times! Even today the Arab loose garment has the same simple look about it.

No doubt this 'drawing together' did originate in Arabia, from whence so many other things have found their way all over the world.

Double Crochet is only to hitch, using 2 threads and looping between them.

With the aid of a hook using two threads the skull cap (*see full colour illustration*) was made.

Without the use of any chain, the entry being between the two upright bars of the stitch, the finished fabric with that stocking stitch look.

Making a circle of string the stitches were worked onto it, with no slip stitch to join the round, a continuation into the first stitch. To decrease the simple method of missing a stitch was used, and when completed the string was pulled out, leaving a selvedge at the bottom.

When recreating this cap the work became very tedious, not only did it want to twist till four rows has been completed, our modern hook seemed inadequate. Perhaps those first hooks had sharper points at the end.

The Matico Indians of North Argentina made bags and pouches in this method, a sample of which can be seen at the Pitts River Museum.

Primitive people use anything around them to aid the production of goods for daily use. Thorns of all kinds are used in many ways; no doubt their crochet hook would have been a thorn.

How simple it is to make a garment in one piece without a seam using this method.

The first circle for the neck, working twice into the same place to form an increase, till a yoke wide enough to cover the shoulders was formed. That round yoke, often used in many babies garments today. From each side of this a smaller circle taken down to form the two sleeves, the larger circle left to make the body. A Sac could also have been made in hitching, which would have taken far longer to make.

Working in the one stitch, the fabric will helix. Introducing one chain gives a type of rib and also helps to give a straight appearance. (See band on Phorahs hat).

Years before irons were invented, many garments were pegged and stretched, which did the same thing as an iron. Under pressing the modern way, the helix of this fabric will only straighten to a point.

By the time of the King Solomon's knot much more would have been known about the individual threads and stitches.

From here would have developed the idea of keeping the loops on the hook, and entering through different ones, bringing us Tunisian crochet, with its form of casting on and casting off.

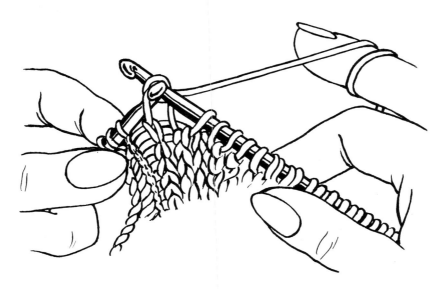

Fig. 35 *Use of 2nd Needle*

When working the second entry as shown, the fabric returns to the stocking stitch look, with the back like a thick purl.

Watching a German woman at her knitting, and seeing her manipulation of the needles, shows how the second hook would have been introduced. Instead of casting off from the left, a looping, taking stitches from the right hook, retaining them on the left. The results—knitting as we know it today, and the stocking stitch. Continental knitters still work all from the front, right to left and left to right, without turning.

With this type of stocking stitch, the fabric would be much finer, using less yarn, and from the front would have the same appearance.

After working in a continuous round with the first craft known, the idea of adding extra needles would quickly have developed.

"Drawing together" and how it began. With one hook, the stitches, Double crochet, chain and Tunisian, adding a second hook, giving knit and purl. At this same time the hooks could have been removed to make a point at the end.

Lastly treble, so much like the twisted single hitch of the stone age man, which does not seem to be known till early nineteenth century. Perhaps this came from France together with the modern name.

In all mass-produced Knitwear, and the very first knitting machine invented, the needles are all small hooks.

Two crafts, from the same source, are sisters. So much alike and so very different.